(larg-

finding

lily

RICHARD CLEWES

to CALLIN MULLIN

*Richard Clewes.
@
Toronto
Harbourfront
Reading Series*

KEY PORTER BOOKS

Library and Archives Canada Cataloguing in Publication

Clewes, Richard
Finding Lily / Richard Clewes.

ISBN 1-55263-745-X

1. Clewes, Richard. 2. Bereavement—Psychological aspects. 3. Self-actualization
(Psychology). I. Title.

BF637.L53C53 2006   155.9'37'092   C2005-905996-6

THE CANADA COUNCIL | LE CONSEIL DES ARTS
FOR THE ARTS | DU CANADA
SINCE 1957 | DEPUIS 1957

ONTARIO ARTS COUNCIL
CONSEIL DES ARTS DE L'ONTARIO

The publisher gratefully acknowledges the support of the Canada Council for the Arts
and the Ontario Arts Council for its publishing program. We acknowledge the support of
the Government of Ontario through the Ontario Media Development Corporation's
Ontario Book Initiative.

We acknowledge the financial support of the Government of Canada through the Book
Publishing Industry Development Program (BPIDP) for our publishing activities.

Key Porter Books Limited
Six Adelaide Street East, Tenth Floor
Toronto, Ontario
Canada M5C 1H6

www.keyporter.com

Text design: Ingrid Paulson
Electronic formatting: Jean Lightfoot Peters

Printed and bound in Canada

06 07 08 09 10 5 4 3 2 1

TO BEN MCNALLY

Canada 49

❝ NOBODY CAN EVER TELL YOU
WHO THEY ARE,
THEY CAN ONLY TELL YOU
WHO THEY WERE ❞

ALAN WATTS

Table of Contents

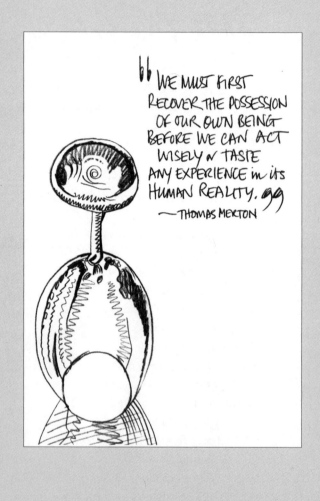

"WE MUST FIRST
RECOVER THE POSSESSION
OF OUR OWN BEING
BEFORE WE CAN ACT
WISELY n TASTE
ANY EXPERIENCE in its
HUMAN REALITY."
— THOMAS MERTON

Introduction

IT WASN'T MY PLAN to write a book about what happened after
my wife took her own life a few days after missing my fiftieth
birthday. I'm an advertising art director, not a storyteller. It's a
noble idea to document the pain and confusion that follows suicide survivors or to give an account of how bravely Erin
grappled with manic depression but this is not my story, one
that I could never have imagined experiencing, much less writing. Until I stopped working, bought a sketchbook, a diary and a
round-the-world plane ticket, I thought I knew myself and what
it might take to resume my life. But it turns out I was wrong on
both counts.

Surviving suicide isn't any more ennobling than stuffing a
million dollars in your bank account. Bipolar disorder is not only
a mental illness, it's a caustic substance. It can dissolve your marriage, your career, your life savings or your favourite person on
the planet as if these things had never existed. In my case, I lost
them all.

Therapy, family, a diary, and the passage of time guided me
and offered indispensable clues about Erin's life and her exit

from it. I learned that no one can control events much less the actions of another person—and that this is okay. Yet I sensed that until I dug deeper into my own life, I would never locate its *animus*. And unless I did I would just be picking up where I left off. I wanted meaning—and a truer life—wherever that took me. I was ready, but not prepared. Like a child wanting to run outside again after a long illness, who is stopped in his tracks by the unexpected view of a strange, new neighbourhood beyond his front door. I needed a better compass and new landmarks. But until I acquired them—which is my story—I did what a lot of people do when their mind is elsewhere, I started doodling.

After a gap of thirty years, I picked up a pen and started to draw. I drew the diary. I drew the room of the house I was renting where I kept the diary. I drew self-portraits. I drew pictures of everything in sight. The fear that my technique wasn't good enough, or that only a real artist would do such a thing, couldn't withstand my rapidly filling sketchbooks. An irresistible urge to compare notes about life with people I didn't know in places I'd never seen became the impetus I needed to pass through the open door.

So the day after Christmas 2003, I traded my old life for a three-month trip around the world. This is the story of finding new "landmarks" in the West Indies, Europe, Asia, Australia, and New Zealand. In rain forests and street corners, airplanes and cafés, glaciers and cabs, from mountain tops to the bottom of the world—wherever I was—I carried a sketchbook/journal. I created postcards, added stamps with a cancellation of the time and place whenever something stirred the needle of my new compass. I mailed the postcards to myself.

People who've seen the postcards have said, "I didn't know you could draw. I didn't know you could write." I didn't know I could either. And if I missed that part about me what else was there to discover?

" IF YOU DON'T KNOW HOW TO LIVE, WHY WONDER ABOUT DEATH? "
— CONFUCIUS

Dead Reckoning

The picture itself is just the tip of the iceberg.

—Sebastiao Salgado, *Photographer*

LESS THAN AN HOUR AGO, a Detective Brand called me on my cell phone, on the way to work, the first day of decent weather. It's spring, finally. I was feeling good for the first time in months—blue sky, warming sun through the sunroof—then the phone chime. I was thinking about the client presentation. I was thinking: thank God for work. Detective Brand identified himself as being from Erin's mother's town and said he had Erin's purse. Did I know where Erin was? She was at her mother's condo and I gave him the number. When had I last spoken to her? I told him we'd separated a few months ago—in case he thought I shouldn't retrieve the purse—but two days ago she called me. She used to call me ten times a day.

I could tell by his pauses, something wasn't right. They didn't know where Erin was. And it looks like I'm going to miss my meeting picking up after her yet again. I clearly remember my last conversation with Erin and exactly what I was thinking. Just yesterday. About her on-again, off-again decision to close her store, leave town, move back to the city. There's a fixable space she likes in a scruffy neighbourhood, but perfect for a new store. And it has an upstairs apartment. "That sounds great, Erin," I'd said, realizing she was manic. In the décor world, she's famous. If anyone can rise again, she can. But I worried this latest idea would cost more than our settlement. And after she's spent her half of the equity in the house, then where will she be? Or me? I managed to stay sort of calmly professional, as if I was reading one of my voice-over scripts. I had the presence of mind to say her enthusiasm was normal.

Normal? Nothing's normal. The house is sold, our marriage is over, and we're separated and broke. I can't imagine how I'm going to deal with the repercussions of financial support. Our bank manager tells me I should at least stop funding the store. He's concerned I'm going to bankrupt myself. "Are we doing the right thing?" Erin had asked me. "Yes," I said. It's done. "It's bad right now, but you'll be okay. We'll both be okay." I almost meant it, too. So when the highway split came into view, one ramp to the city, the other to the suburbs, I was thinking, "I guess I better go get her purse and here we go again. Another day being changed by Erin's behaviour."

In Detective Brand's special room drained of colour there's a painting of an alpine lake hanging on the wall, an insipid carpet covering the floor, an armchair and thickly upholstered couch, and I am thinking, "This can't be good." I have never been in a police station before. There are no phones on the side tables, just boxes of tissue. And silence. As if all unnecessary sounds are being deliberately retrieved, sucked into the furnishings.

"Please sit." It's the voice on the phone. Efficient, neutral.

"Oh, God," I say. Now I understand. Please. Don't say anything more. But he continues in an almost peaceful tone that makes no sense because—can he not see?—I am shaking, shivering, my insides shifting like plates about to spill out of my hands.

"Richard, your wife's body was found at two o'clock this morning," he is saying slowly, his eyes locked on me. The meaning is perfectly clear but still I cling to the words from the telephone call: her purse. I thought I was here about Erin's purse?

"I am sorry," continues Detective Brand, "but Erin took her own life. She jumped from her mother's balcony."

I understand what I am hearing but that can't be.

"Where was her mother? Is her mother there?" I say. What possible difference does that make? Didn't you hear the man? Erin is gone.

"Erin was alone. We thought you might know where to reach her mother. The neighbours didn't know," says Detective Brand.

"The neighbours found her?" I ask Detective Brand.

"Yes," he says.

I think I know the answer to his question but all I say is, "Oh, God. This can't be happening." But it is and we just keep talking.

"I'm sorry," says Detective Brand and I can see he means it, or it looks like he does, and now realize I haven't answered the question.

"She must be at Erin's sister's place, babysitting." I say. Oh, God. They don't know. I'm going to have to tell them.

"Was there any kind of note?" I ask.

"No."

"Where is she?"

"At the hospital. Do you know how to get there?"

"Yes."

Detective Brand says he's sorry again and gives me a business card, which strikes me as strange for a policeman, and I hold on to it as if it's worth something and he says this must be very hard but could I please go to the hospital? For the identification.

So I still have a purpose.

Now I am in the hospital lobby where, strangely, everyone is wearing a mask: the Indian man in the kiosk selling coffee and newspapers, the sick and the not-so-sick waiting in hard plastic chairs, the ambulance attendants pushing the gurney, the nurses, people in white coats, patients leaving for a smoke, towing small children (who have pushed their masks on the top of their heads like party hats) or iv drips on stands. Everyone's in masks.

What is going on here?

Now I see the posted signs in English, French, and Mandarin. Have I got a cough? Have I recently been in China, Vietnam, or Singapore? It's SARS. The epidemic has forced all hospitals to take emergency measures. This is an emergency.

How true.

But an epidemic isn't going to stop this. I must see Erin and later I will have to find Erin's mother and her sisters. I feel like someone else is operating my movements.

I wash my hands with the special soap that evaporates before you can work up lather. I'm looking for the information counter. I pull the mask around my face and pinch the metal tab over my nose to keep it on. As if any of this mattered. A guy in blue scrubs has pointed me to the information desk. I want to take off this stupid mask, but I have to keep it on, be like everybody else.

Can't anyone see how much pain I'm in, how afraid I am? I need help. Help me, somebody.

"Where is the morgue office, please?" I mumble to a volunteer at Patient Enquiry and she directs me with a turn of her gauzed face, down the hall. At the second door on the right, which is open a crack, I knock and enter.

"I'm here to identify my wife," I say to a middle-aged woman in a white lab coat sitting behind a computer. She looks up. The room is so quiet I hear her mouse clicking.

"What is her name?" she asks. I tell her. Panic is thickening into dread, getting heavier by the second. Now I recognize that I do not want to see Erin's body. This is happening too fast. This is not how Erin and I were supposed to part. Suddenly, I realize when wives die husbands are always suspected first; maybe Detective Brand only wanted to check me out. Is this some kind of test?

Slowly the morgue clerk flips pages trapped in a clipboard with one hand, spins and flicks her mouse with the other, her eyes never leaving the screen.

"She isn't here. Are you sure?" she says. Click. Flip. Click.

What's that? Am *I* sure?

"I'm sure. Please look again," I say mustering as much patience as I can manage. This is not directory assistance for crissakes. This is my wife—or my former wife—a woman I loved once and gave everything to, who then threw it all away and after that, herself.

"No, there's no one here with that name." That peculiar silence again. Like the moment before Detective Brand spoke.

The clerk sees me making a move for the door and picks up her desk phone.

"It's alright. Use your cell phone." Click. Flip. Click.

I have Detective Brand's card, dial his direct line. He's not there. At lunch. Punch zero.

"Look," I say to a new female voice, "He told me she was at this hospital and she is not. Where is she? Can you find out?" How do you lose a dead person?

No one knows. It's not the receptionist's fault, of course. It is not anyone's fault. It is not Erin's fault. Whose, I wonder?

Just then another woman with grey-streaked plain-cut hair enters the room. She tells me her name, which I cannot make out, but I see the crucifix on her lapel. She is the hospital chaplain. I pull off my mask. She takes her mask off, too.

"What did you say?" I say to her.

"I said, there is no need for you to be here. Erin is here. The body has already been positively identified."

The bubble has burst.

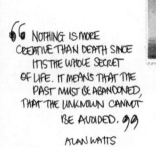

" NOTHING IS MORE
CREATIVE THAN DEATH SINCE
IT IS THE WHOLE SECRET
OF LIFE. IT MEANS THAT THE
PAST MUST BE ABANDONED,
THAT THE UNKNOWN CANNOT
BE AVOIDED. "

ALAN WATTS

Let's Do Some Living After We Die

EXPERIENCE IS BESIDE THE POINT when you start a diary. I've told myself many things about Erin since her death. My mind is an obnoxious talk radio host that won't take another caller. I don't know how else to tune into the source of her decision—or banish it—so I write. No matter what, I have to get this truth-telling right. But can I really be defense lawyer and prosecutor?

Just tell the truth.

I am accompanied only by my well-educated, veracity-challenged, self-absorbed intellect. Together, we picked out the thickest, leather-bound journal in a stationery store. I've finally put to use a drawing pen with an ink cartridge given to me by my nephew for my fiftieth birthday.

No matter how odd, contradictory or sad, I record these internal dialogues—conversations between me and me. I need to, before my imagination gets a hold of them. There's nothing I can do now about the fact I sold an idealized version of life to myself, one indisputably at odds with reality, even as Erin's depression dug its heels in. Too late. Focus on the clues. *Cherchez la femme.*

Erin's gone. Where did you last see yourself?

I've never revealed anything more introspective than an article in a trade journal on the subject of starting an ad agency. Which I later lost. I am a creative person. I'm only as good as my last assignment. I stopped thinking advertising was art a long time ago. I've been self-employed for more than twelve years. I have re-invented myself umpteen times. I know what it takes to survive, professionally at least. You just get out there again and bang away. It's a risky profession that pays well. It built our dream house and financed Erin's store. There's always a trade off.

I realize, with a terrible shock, that I've spent my life putting a thing in the best light, placing this word on top of that image. Except for a couple of years teaching high school, it's all I've ever done. Mutual funds, beer, a television network, a muffler-shop chain, a couple of hospital foundations, a diet cola, accountants, German cars, Italian computers, and a Canadian bank. These are the stories I write about. I don't know my own story or even if I care to know it.

You must find out what really happened.

The Diary

It is often thought that the dead see us. And we assume, whether reasonably or not, that if they see at all they see us more clearly than before.

—C.S. Lewis, *A Grief Observed*

I write.

MAY 11

I could say my profession acclimatized me to look at the world as it really is—and provide a new and improved perspective instead. But that's not completely true—it's in my nature to idealize. The worse Erin's mental state became, the more determined I was to manipulate the explanation of her condition to my family and friends and myself. It was clever, the way I did it. I simply denied anything awful was happening. Especially to me—that was the key. I saw Erin's mania and depression—and how it emptied bank accounts and vaporized love—and managed to look right through it. I don't say I didn't feel its sting; just that I gawked at depression's fury. The way you gaze at footage of floods, hurricanes, and tsunami disasters on TV or slow down to take a good look at a car accident. In this case, I was more than an innocent bystander. I don't think my eyes can be trusted now. As far as seeing the future, they're more likely to provide false testimony than a fresh perspective. I have to speak to someone. But who will listen to a man as foolish as me?

MAY 12

People criticize advertising for its shallowness but that doesn't begin to go deep enough. Beneath the thin layer separating consciousness from cash registers, there is, frankly, nothing at all. Advertising is about making one particular moment last forever. Messages charged with cultural nuance neatly packed into shiny little boxes (or flat screens). I've spent more time worrying about what happens in thirty seconds than in my own life. I'm grateful to be working and the distraction of the past month has been good, but can I stay in this real world? Making ads is the only thing that keeps me aloft; it's been like living in the calm centre of a hurricane. If there is relief out there, I doubt I'd be able to see it. What I know is this: those who don't keep up professionally get whipsawed. That kind of thinking encouraged me to feed the store with money.

I never saw Erin's storm coming.

MAY 13

A well-intentioned accountant friend who deals with divorce settlements suggested my situation is better than it could be. Maybe he's right. Maybe I'd resent making support payments to Erin for the rest of my life. That's one of those "what ifs" and I have too many of them already. The depression slowly drained my love for her and, I must believe, she realized I hung in anyway. For her? For me? It's complicated. I keep reminding myself: we were separated and heading for divorce.

MAY 14

You couldn't help but love Erin. Everyone did. She possessed a genuine warmth and easy way with friends or total strangers. Despite her struggle to hold on to mental equilibrium, she displayed grace almost to the end. I felt lucky when I first met her and I still do. For all the baubles and trinkets of the modern, middle-class, overachieving lifestyle that she sold in her store, Erin had no pretensions that possessions conferred status or happiness. The spas, the shopping sprees, the dinners—they were narcissistic gestures out of her normal character. But, over the last two years, I subsidized the store to the edge of personal bankruptcy while buying her gifts that were way over-the-top. Who was sicker?

MAY 24

The moving van arrives tomorrow. I think I see now that my intention with money was as much to distract the pandemonium in Erin's head as to make myself feel better. Her depression was a mobile, 24/7 vortex pulling everything into a thick chaos. Erin's sharply swinging mood ruled our days. If up, I stayed out of the way, letting her deflate, as she did eventually. If down, I actually got stuff done. That was the working theory at least. It didn't always delineate itself so neatly, but it helped me avoid walking on pins and needles all the time. Tonight, I wandered around the property and circled our house one last time. So many buried dreams and secrets. It was like walking through the killing fields.

MAY 26

Thank God for my friends. Last night, they brought dinner and housewarming presents to this new place, a cabin I've decided to rent in the village. Being with them without Erin reminded me of all those dinner parties when she cooked an elaborate meal and we tried to have a "normal night." This morning I listened to the peal of the church bell, quite loud and just a block away. Somewhere along the line, we stopped attending. Instead, I used to lie in bed at night and pray before going to sleep and once I noticed Erin did, too.

MAY 27

There was no one to talk to about it. What was going on with Erin was a secret we kept so well we didn't breathe a word of it to one another. We were so good; the obfuscation became a kind of remedy. Occasionally, when we saw Erin's therapist, it was possible to admit to the presence of depression but after a few days, things returned to—I was about to write—normal. Actually, we'd go back to saying as little as possible about the Heavy Thing. We thought we'd made some progress the last time we saw Leslie together. Our last appointment was September 11, 2001.

MAY 25

About twice a year, always during a manic phase, I warned Erin she was drifting away. As if she didn't know that. I blurted out, "Your references aren't to this marriage." How pompous I must have sounded. As if maybe she'd misplaced her marriage, her feelings towards me and who she used to be. And, of course, that was all true.

JUNE 1

The weirdest part of bipolar mood disorder is that while its victims swing back and forth, spouses try to keep their own head from being chopped off by the emotional pendulum. When she was at the bottom, it was impossible to get mad at Erin. But it wasn't unthinkable to lash back at her during a manic phase. Of course, I regret losing my temper. My frustration couldn't have pushed her any farther away, but then maybe in her mind my reaction justified her dramatic exits. She'd blow out the door in a whirl of righteous indignation and check into a hotel downtown and crank up the credit card. A day later she'd come home as if nothing had happened. Anger, guilt, worry, and exhaustion: this was the cycle, probably for both of us. I let her disappearances go. What else could I do? Nothing was going to fix Erin or our future together. Depression tore up the marriage and ripped our finances apart. Despite this, I thought the important thing was to carry right on, demonstrate loyalty to a bygone time in our relationship.

JUNE 2

I couldn't "read" Erin when she was alive, so why am I trying now? The power of depression to crowd out her personality was truly stunning. I lost track of it—of her. I carried the responsibility for keeping up appearances but no one asked me to. As fast as I cancelled her cards, she'd get a new one through work and run it past its limit. So the question is this: If I'd had the financial means to keep up with Erin's "buying trips" to Atlanta and New York, could I have placated her, saved her, slowed her down at all? Given enough money, would she still be alive today? Would I even want to be with her? So many secrets, all of them carried away, out there in the night.

Don't be afraid to find out.

JUNE 3

I wake up every night at exactly the same time: 2 AM. Last night—or I guess it's this morning—I thought: I tried to compete with her mood disorder. Maybe if it appeared to Erin that we were a normal couple, or capable of a normal life, she'd recognize my support and choose to come back. But to Erin, all the signs and markers of a normal life were written in an unintelligible language. Now I'm wondering if the signs were so good, why can't *I* see them anymore. I need my own landmarks. Home's long gone.

JUNE 4

I was looking at my feet for what seemed like several hours today. I moved them only to move the shadow. It made me think in the end the surface became the only substance in my life. The big house, the popular store, our social life—these were dazzling props in our facsimile world. These things are meaningless. I'm embarrassed even to point this out.

JUNE 5

Am I angry that I lost it all? My best friend asked me that today and I didn't know what to say. It's not what I feel. I'm not angry at Erin for killing herself and I don't really care to keep the house even if I could afford it. The thing is, her life, my life, our home became so tangled up I can't separate any of it. So I'm relieved. What *does* make me angry are the people who come up to me in the grocery store and say, in a confidential whisper, how worried they were about all the weight Erin lost. Invigorated by seeing me standing over the lettuce, they shoot me this look of restrained disapproval. They want to say, "Didn't you notice it, Rick?" Why don't they just say so and be done with it? If they did I might feel better for hearing such stupidity.

JUNE 6

The question really is: how did Erin and I know to pick each other ten years earlier? The precision is mind-blowing. If we'd never met, what then? Would she still be alive? I am weary of so much self-awareness. I have to lie down almost every day around 2 PM for an hour or so. I can't seem to put in a full work day without a nap.

JUNE 6. AGAIN.

Erin would know how to decorate this place. When I met her she lived in a tiny apartment, decorated within an inch of its life. When I met her she was doing just fine. I screwed her up.

JUNE 7

I am restless and yet I just sit here after dinner until the sun goes down. It feels like this feeling inside will last forever. Not despair, not fear, just a profound emptiness. And an utter lack of perspective on "my loss." Loss? It's more like extinction.

JUNE 8

I don't feel abandoned by God but I'd be interested to see what He's been up to outside these four walls. No water again. I have to decide if I want a shower or do laundry. I can't do both without losing the prime on the well.

JUNE 11

Two months and our tenth wedding anniversary. I have learned that up to 10 percent of people with depression attempt suicide. I rejected joining a suicide survivor group. There's an organization downtown that starts groups every six weeks. How's that for tragic? I need to know the secret that explains not why Erin took her life but why I've been left behind to deal with it. I couldn't finish the last book on suicide; I need a spiritual explanation. I understand Erin jumped off her mother's apartment balcony because she couldn't stand another day living with her brain. These books are as ineffectual as Erin regarded her drugs, therapy or my pep talks about the store and her health.

JUNE 12

I've started weekly sessions with a therapist. At first, I approached appointments as if Marion was a skeptical client I had to win over with a really good creative concept. And I made a conscious effort to be likeable. I talked about Erin as if Marion was a colleague and we were having a fascinating chat about the worst thing we'd ever heard of. It began to gnaw at me. Then, after a particularly bad sleep and the 2 AM drink of water at the kitchen sink, I "heard" a voice that said:

Stop putting on a good face.

JUNE 15

I don't know what frightens me more: hearing a voice within me, or the realization that it might know what it's talking about. I am too tired to fight this weird development.

The truth is the truth is an acquired taste.

JULY 1

In the car today, I found an undeveloped roll of film. I had the pictures printed and the first one is of Erin wearing a suede coat, smiling on a fall day. What was she thinking at that moment? Have I ever known? I put the photo on the coffee table then surrounded it with more pictures of everyone in my family. This is getting harder. You cannot "happy up" a depressed person. It's just as useless for survivors of suicide.

JULY 4
I see I am writing a lot about how tough the depression was on me. Just saying that somehow seems disrespectful of Erin. What saves me from becoming some kind of sad-looking "War with Depression" vet is keeping these feelings to myself. Whatever I am going through is so much easier than Erin's trials when she was alive. I don't know how Erin coped with her blackness. I can reasonably hope my inner voice isn't interested in self-annihilation.

JULY 5
Two days before she died, Erin called me and talked about returning to our marriage. Her voice had become profoundly detached and monotone. Her story sounded like she was talking about some couple we knew slightly. Or maybe she was letting me go by showing how unfixable she had become. My response surprised me. I was gentle but circumspect. Another kind of detachment. I feared my words were loaded with danger. I said, "You've done the right thing. You should pursue your instinct to move back to the city." Erin had more than enough talent to work for the best décor retailers. I reminded her of her reputation and following. As usual, I couldn't tell if she'd heard me. I wonder if I wasn't cutting her last connection to the real world.

JULY 17
Three months, six days. I measure the time since, as if it mattered. This morning I can't shake the guilt. Guilt is an intoxicating drink you pour yourself to take the edge off the false

complicity. A wallop of self-pity chased with a hope to be let off the hook. What if I'd known more about Ativan, Effexor or Paxil? Had I even done an adequate job monitoring her medication? What if I'd been able to stop her going to her mother's apartment? She would have been forty-four today.

AUGUST 11

Four months. I want to believe that Erin would have gotten better had she lived. Some days, she knew how far she had travelled from normal life. Some days, I felt like the character in the movie who realizes too late that the car ignition is rigged to a bomb just as the innocent driver turns the key. How do you get closure on that? Closure is a fantasy.

SEPTEMBER 11

Five months. Erin alone formed the decision to take her life. It is a conceit to think otherwise, but I have had to re-read my diary several times this week, at 2 AM and now also at 4 AM. There is no logic to her distorted, independent act. But, if that's true, then there's nothing to get my arms around. Erin's sister Sherry is pregnant with their first. Mom complains of chest pains.

OCTOBER 31

Halloween. All Souls' Eve. Leaves are well off the trees. I've been watching the burning hulks of cars left by suicide bombers in Iraq on CNN all night. The only thing that might make possible sense: What if the soul is life's continuity? Would that make it an ejector seat, carrying your essence away from death to somewhere else, a safer place? I've never thought much about life after death. I've never taken the time to consider if it's worth fearing. To take your own life, that's fearful. And the horrifying part is I keep absorbing her suicide like these CNN reports. After a while, I numb to it but twenty-four hours later it's fresh again. Breaking news: Erin gone forever. It's odd, but stranger is the recognition of an internal presence that seems to be tuned into everything I'm thinking.

NOVEMBER 11

My clients are terrific but I can't keep this pace up much longer. How do you take a leave of absence from yourself? I have to admit I have no idea what to do next. So much for the high-functioning individual Marion is always talking about. I keep thinking about just stopping, leaving. Maybe a trip around the world.

DECEMBER 11

I blurted out the idea of a break to a client today who said I'd been talking about a trip for weeks.

DECEMBER 13

Went to my mother's for a pre-Christmas get-together with brothers and sisters and their kids. Love is noisy. On the way home, I had to turn off the Christmas songs and concentrate on the road.

DECEMBER 14

Dave and Eddie have been married five months today. It was Erin who set them up. I could barely make it through the toasts to the bride. Last summer seems like last century. Erin's employees sat at my table watching for my reaction. I miss my house. I miss Erin, any version of her. I miss my life.

DECEMBER 15

I bought the ticket.

Self Storage

How much death works,
No one knows what a long
Day he puts in. The little
Wife always alone
Ironing death's laundry.
                    —Charles Simic, "Eyes Fastened With Pins"

In all, I've kept four of everything, plates, glasses, and cutlery. Every time I open a drawer or cupboard in this miniscule place I wonder why I'm keeping the extra three.

I boxed up things I wouldn't need again like crystal wine glasses, wedding albums, and Christmas decorations and put them in storage. On the advice of my brother, I held on to the TV. "You never know," Brian said. As he hooked up the satellite I imagined the secret to Erin's downfall being tonight's theme on the

Shopping Channel. I gave him the Crate & Barrel leather chairs for his cottage. My friend Peter reluctantly accepted the garden tools and hose caddies plus the BBQ; he tells me every time we talk that I can have them back whenever I want. The twelve-foot dining table and arrowback chairs, I threw into the garage sale of what was left of Erin's store and gave the proceeds to a mental health organization. It didn't help particularly. Hundreds of her books on perfect home décor went to the town library. I crammed a three-yard dumpster with stuff like cushions, pillows, rattan baskets. I emptied the basement and swept out the garage. I cried. Gord, the guy who plowed our road, stopped by just as I was at the nose-blowing stage. I would have thrown away two winters' worth of firewood into the treeline but Gord was happy to haul it away. The house is emptier now than when we moved in six years ago.

Sherry packed up Erin's clothes and I returned to her all of her sister's childhood photos. I thought about keeping one of Erin on a pony at six or seven years old. She was a gorgeous kid. With her white blond hair and thin nose, she looked happy and comfortable, like she'd been born riding but I remember the story she told me: a guy walked through the subdivision, one street after another, with the pony and a camera, and mothers plunked their kids into the saddle.

There were things I shouldn't have pitched, that I could have saved for a day when they'll be needed but I can't imagine that day. I'd had enough of being the museum guard to our marriage. Living alone in the house, waiting for the sale to close, was like moving into a funeral home after the visitation. I was angry, too. What I wanted was to put an end to the place but Erin had already seen to that.

That was nine months ago. Now I'm packing again only this time it's a suitcase.

I'm leaving my lime green cabin for parts unknown. It's been a good hideout for almost a year but I need to be out chasing the secret.

The cabin roof practically touches the old Methodist church next door where my landlords live. He's a mechanic and she cuts hair on Thursdays in what used to be the minister's vestry. It would be nice if God would throw me a bone, down to one of His former properties. Between two old cedars I will extract my car tomorrow morning. It's the weekend so there will be the accountants on Harleys starting at dawn. As vehicles make the sharp right turn, headlights will illuminate the entire cabin interior. It's been like living in a lighthouse but in reverse. Which is funny; driving back from meetings in the city, this was the landmark that said I was home.

I doubt that any process—getting rid of things, staying here indefinitely, or going on this trip around the world—will shake the grief. Grief is a shadow that follows me everywhere. It's sticky and always underfoot. No matter where my thoughts run, I cannot stay stranded anymore between what happened and what's next.

TUESDAY.

Grief is a stickler for details with an insatiable appetite. It's a subtle, relentless authority, like being interrogated by a border guard—except I'm providing both sides of the interview. And why the third degree? I'm trying to get out of, not into the country. After nine months, I've learned there's no special preparation for meaning—certainly no incremental peace but I've shown up each day. I accommodate grief. It's just, I have to say, grief's an ungrateful guest.

Just before I moved, I got a call from Erin's therapist. We hadn't spoken since the funeral. It was an odd moment because when the phone rang I happened to be looking at the photograph album of Erin's fortieth birthday party. There's one of Erin and her friend Eddie, deep in conversation. We'd just moved into the house that spring; as a surprise, I'd rented a limo for the day and we'd been in Manhattan. I said: buy anything you want and, naturally, she bought nothing. I can still hear the hired jazz trio, the bleat of the saxophone, the smoky aroma of rosemary on lamb chops, the feel of the wind. The photographs show us as the happy couple that I thought we were.

During the call, the therapist said that Erin had never demonstrated any "insight into her depression." I know she meant that as a consoling balm. She also reminded me of Erin's father and grandmother, and of their own histories of depression. So what?

If Erin had understood why she was so bleak would death have turned its back? Are we only a genetic apparatus interacting with a personal set of neurological functions? My instinct says the loss of our savings because of the store, the need to sell the dream house, the broken marriage, the suicide—the whole rotten mess—didn't just happen. It evolved. Things went wrong, day after day. Once, in the shower, after a particularly manic time during a weekend with clients, I formed a perverse wish: why doesn't she just die? When Erin was down, I leapt into action, managing the house, our finances and my work in a frenzy all my own. Where was my insight? Was I evil to have said that? What is insight anyway?

WEDNESDAY.
It's hard to stay focused on self-discovery when the smoke detector keeps going off even when I boil water, which is ironic because that's as much involvement with the stove as I can tolerate these days. Microwaveable lasagnas, take-out sushi and

pizza—I eat dinner over the kitchen sink. In fact, the faster I can get through food, the better. I don't like being reminded that I once enjoyed cooking.

THURSDAY.

At 6 AM I shower and shave. Fifty push-ups, two hundred sit-ups. I make coffee, pour multivitamins, cereal and grapefruit juice down my throat, and then walk to the general store for the paper. Run, work, sleep. Not necessarily in that order but seven days a week. Shaving is new; for twenty years a beard hid my face. I wanted to look older. I succeeded.

In addition to shaving, I'm meditating, which is a way—for a blessed half-hour each day—to deny a live studio audience the constant chatter in my head.

I haven't read a book in several years. Now I'm plowing through three a week: Po Bronson's *What Should I Do With My Life?*, Dr. Thomas Lewis's *A General Theory of Love*, and *Eyewitness Guide to New Zealand*. My notes string together a mid-life crisis, "limbic regulation," and how to book space on the Milford Track.

I like the ritual of cleaning. It gives me a small sense of control, which I know is pointless. I sweep the kitchen floor and vacuum the living room one last time, particularly the carpeting at the front door where Alex the pizza guy—a real Italian, from Venice—will stand tonight to get out of the weather, if it's still snowing. There's no vestibule; you just walk in from the road onto the carpet. Alex doesn't know to come around the side, to the kitchen door. I never use the front door or turn on the outdoor light. Alex will smile as he always does as if to say he's as baffled as I am and all one can do is hope for the best. Sometimes I can't believe that life just keeps tripping along. Pizza delivery has been very reassuring.

Once a week, I bundle the garbage and put out the recycling. Sometimes there is nothing to bundle. Then, I take my clothes to Estelle's laundromat in the village. It's near Marion's office. I call it "Clothes & Brain Washing Day." Estelle opens at 8:30 AM but people know she's in an hour before that. Her coffee is better than mine and I pass the time reading *New Yorker* magazines.

When I drive I have a chance to think. Reading Estelle's magazines gave me the following cartoon idea. Death sits in an office being interviewed by a serious HR type. He asks Death a question from a psychological survey, oblivious to the drapery and scythe. The caption is: "Would you say you work to live or live to work?"

The answer is: death's indifferent.

Not aloof but inhuman. What makes suicide such a breathtaking event is that death isn't supposed to be self-inflicted. Suicide is permanently mysterious. More frightening than ordinary death and more *verboten* even than money. A few people I thought I knew better have avoided the subject of Erin's death as if they think death has now been brought closer to their lives because it's been close to someone they can say they know. As if suicide was a contagion. They don't want death loitering around their front doors and I don't blame them. In truth, death is comfortably parked inside their corporal homes, the ultimate stale date stamped on every cell. That's why suicides offend. Erin forced fate to play its hand prematurely. She changed the lives of everyone who ever cared for her while depression, the cause, skulked away. Statements like "You only live once" and "I could be hit by a bus tomorrow" deflect criticism of that extravagant vacation or expensive new car, but such explanations don't constitute a deep enough awareness of death's influence and importance. As a society, we should probably think about death more. But maybe not as much as I have been.

I've been to the kitchen sink three times tonight. All I know is life's messy—probably on purpose. The cliché goes: death is part of life, but my metaphysical contribution is that neither is particularly correlative any more than an empty stadium on the day after the World Series can tell you who won or lost. Death is final and unequivocal while life's one damn thing after another. Life requires imagination. And so does death. Response–wise, you make it up on the spot. You have to be flexible and creative in responding to random setbacks or full-blown horrors and, most of all, the pure uncertainty of being alive.

In the end, death wasn't Erin's problem; it was her solution, which has made death my newest advertising client. I say, re-position it.

First, let's admit: Death's perfect. It's the leading brand in a one-product category. It has zero competition. Death doesn't need constant re-introduction, either. It will never display a corner flash that says: "Now With More Grief."

We are all shoppers and Death's waiting patiently at the cash-out counter. I am pissed about the customer who barged through my line without paying. No question, I will want to see somebody in charge about Erin.

Suicide is the classic "the customer is always right" scenario.

Nobody's going to stop you, not even God. I imagine Erin was out of her mind the moment she abandoned her shopping cart, glanced at Death and headed for the parking lot. I think they probably knew each other from previous occasions. I don't blame her for thinking about it. So much pain. I could barely cope just living beside the depression.

Let's suppose God decides He wants to tinker with Death's marketing strategy. Eons of complaints received through those smart souls in the marketing group finally persuaded Him; time to take a fresh look at Life's only major weakness—its short-lived product cycle. Customers have been saying all along it's too brief, too random. Ironically, only the suicides are grateful life wasn't longer. Not your best endorsement campaign.

With the hundred thousand years of negative impressions of natural death (we'll set aside suicide stats) maybe Death can be re-positioned. Flavoured more as Hindu or Buddhist and less Judeo–Christian. Get Death out of the whole "you only live once" area and de-emphasize the finality angle. One concept might be to present death as a personality whose traditionally austere nature is really just a cover for a tough entity doing a tough job. Tougher than the Pillsbury Dough Boy, for sure he's actually a pretty good listener with a steady hand. With all kinds of experience in the world between worlds, Death is in no rush and you shouldn't be either. Make sure you got all you wanted out of life, he might have said to Erin.

The important part isn't changing, the marketing people assure God—the Life Store customers are still going to die; we're a monopoly, after all. But God's got to keep up with His increasingly savvy consumers. Humankind is all over cloning small mammals; mortals are determined to de-code and fool with their very own genetic best-before dates. Soon life will be prolonged, and then the life-after-death program will get lost in the shuffle. How will we keep them down on the farm, metaphysically speaking? This is fundamentally a quality issue. The suicides just don't see the quality.

Or we could re-launch Death as a kind of action figure. Life Affirmer (versus the tiresome Grim Reaper). This would give God one last chance with His toughest customers. Time to ditch the hooded figure with the bony finger. WMDS and North Korea are far scarier. The marketing group would like to have every cashier do a little satisfaction survey before they ring suicides through. It won't alienate the natural deaths; their time's up. It might slow down the suicides. And finally (no pun intended) as a replacement for the Big Bright Light all cashiers will hand out large flashlights with a brochure entitled: "Your Heaven, Your Own Light."

The problem with this scenario is suicides already fit the self-service model. They are "early adopters." They are highly motivated but unpredictable. Nowhere in the fertile folds of a suicide's neocortex is there sufficient space for new and improved Death to plant persuasive arguments in favour of post-poning death. There's no point in asking them, "Did you find everything you were looking for?" They did not.

These shoppers are preoccupied with and by an apparatus undergoing constant insurrection. Things were as bad as it could get and then they got much worse. "Satisfaction or your money cheerfully refunded." Too late. They haven't got the slightest interest in speaking to anyone in charge. What they want to do is get even. For all the pain and suffering, they want nothing less than revenge.

SATURDAY. LAST DAY.

I'm coming back from a final client meeting. All the way home, I study the familiar landscape (the office towers, the billboards, the highway traffic, the off-ramp to the suburbs, the farms and wide open spaces), replaying every important stage of my life (school, work, women, marriage, home), not sure what role my choices had in all of it, especially ten years with Erin. At my own end, will I still wonder if I was good enough to her? Did I miss some-thing? Was there a turnoff for a higher purpose I blew past?

SUNDAY MORNING.

Erin's death removed me from the version of life we made, not life itself, but still, I don't think I am quite awake. It's as if I am in the ultimate witness protection program. For my own good, my old identity is gone, but a new one hasn't been worked out yet. I'm a perverse amnesiac—the self I do remember, I don't want back. That person—or maybe just parts of that person—is in self-storage while I take this trip.

I wake up at 2 and 4 AM. I re-read every page of Saturday's paper. On the "Births & Deaths" page, an excruciating bereavement notice stood out from every global calamity. On the twelfth anniversary of his wife's death, the husband's words struck a dreadful tone that sounded recent and inconsolable. They had a bitter edge. I wondered if this was something he did annually, if his emotions or his prose ever varied. I read it over and over, looking for some hint of acceptance or optimism but as far as he was concerned, two people had died that day. He clearly wasn't interested in ditching the grief. It was chilling. I turned on the TV. More pity beaming my way—and a high-grade mix of revulsion and befuddlement, as I watch a news clip of Shiite zealots on a holy day, beating themselves with leather-braided whips, blood streaming down their backs, walking down main street Baghdad as if they were a drum and bugle corps on parade.

Coincidentally, my brother Peter calls my cabin the Hair Shirt Palace.

His unspoken concern has been that I've made it harder on myself than it has to be. By staying in the country and not appearing to be interested in moving back to the city, Peter thinks I've cut myself off. Maybe I have. It's not stubbornness that locks me out, is it? I can't see myself here or there any more than I can tell self-pity from pain. He worries I will torch my career bridge; no one we know has ever taken three months off. Options–wise I'm fresh out. I need this trip. I'm counting the hours.

This past summer, Peter and Mary and I mingled with hundreds of people at the Beaches Jazz Festival. The main street is closed to cars. There's a food stand at every intersection and musical flavours for every taste: Dixieland, bop, fusion, techno, swing. People had a very good time. I felt like I was watching a movie with no subtitles.

In front of a shoe store, a Brillo-haired teenager, a dead ringer for Pat Metheny, wailed on his Stratocaster while an elegant woman twenty-plus years older—his mother, I imagine—smiled beatifically. She swayed and clapped her hands to the beat. Between songs she sold homemade CDs. I catch Mary's eye; we are thinking the same thing. She looks like an older version of Erin; same face, different expression. Except this woman practically radiates joy.

The sun's up, revealing a delicate snowfall. I'm packed: passport, ticket, cash. The limo will be here in an hour. There's nothing left to worry about. If the cabin gets broken into, what will I lose? A TV, my computer?

This time tomorrow, it will be sunny and warm. I can run every day and that alone should give me a lift but I don't feel like a traveller so much as an elaborately packed piece of flotsam and jetsam.

I have been trying to imagine myself one day, after the trip, as happy as the guitarist's mother. It's hard to accept that no one is guaranteed mental health. No one is entitled to happiness, either. Maybe making room for it is all we're expected to do.

Running Out of Territory

Midway in our life's journey, I went astray from the straight road and woke to find myself alone in a dark wood.

—Dante, "Inferno," *The Divine Comedy*

ONE LAST RUN BEFORE the limo arrives. I have run this trail fifty times, looking down as often as ahead; metamorphic claws will tear shoes and grab ankles. There are patches of gel-slick snow lodged under sarcophagus-sized rocks and braided stanchions of cedar. And the Heavy Thing escorts me so I must watch every footfall. I am learning to watch my mind but it is too often clogged with energy and intentions that have nowhere to go. I will need to recruit unknown parts of me for the planned journey because I know so well where I am and even how I got here, every step. In other words, I am completely lost.

Boom, boom, boom.

Running has always been an adjournment from business demands and from secret turmoil. I once persuaded Erin to come with me on a trail not far from here but ten minutes into it, she turned around, having seen enough. Maybe she was uncomfortable with the silence or the immobility of being in a forest, even one as small as this.

She needed to leave her surroundings at a moment's notice. Impulsively she would drop the hose at the foot of the vegetable garden and bolt for her Explorer. I'd get the explanation in a voice-mail: a forgotten appointment with a furniture–maker, a bank deposit before closing, dinner at her sister's. But more often, especially in the mornings, it was an excuse to have a cigarette. The township's retired farmers and landscape crews who assembled at dawn in the Time for Coffee knew the elegant lady with the blonde hair and sunglasses as the owner of the décor store, but they never, Gord told me at the funeral, interrupted her privacy. Gord's crews plowed roads and driveways, trimmed the lawns and trees of all the bigger weekend places and he kept many secrets. His boys shared cigarettes with Erin, he admitted; I thought she'd quit before we got married.

Boom, boom, boom.

Erin claimed that workouts no longer calmed her and in the last three years she'd stopped exercising altogether. Obsessed by errands for work or a grocery list for a dinner party, Erin attempted to distract her mind, but her mind remained in revolt. I smiled at the gentle-looking woman behind the wheel, blowing me a kiss like a visiting dignitary, moving away.

From the road, you won't see the trails that reach out in all directions through the Escarpment like ganglia. Over creeks, down wooded ravines, past hidden ponds, outdoor education centres, dairy pastures, organic farms, hay fields, Christmas tree farms, exhausted quarries, and active gravel pits, trails are deeply hidden furrows jostling with Nature. Nature wants them all back.

It relentlessly works to expunge scars on its variant surface. In a few months, grasses gain astonishing height and grow up to the verge of the trails: rain erases my tracks as it deepens the orange skin of useless tractors, the abandoned harrows, and the shells of defunct cars. The sun blisters the sugar shacks and unpainted fences that demark private property from the bush until everything in Nature's path, even the path itself, will be quietly snared and leisurely collected. An unused trail won't remain a trail for long.

I used to be able to put the Heavy Thing in my backpack on weekend runs with Dave and Peter. They are married, fit, young fathers, and good men. We talked as friends, as husbands, confidently describing the exhilarating and troubling events in our business lives. It was a guilty pleasure to share insights about three particular women. We said less than we knew either out of respect or bewilderment. Once, Peter told me (at the bottom of an unpleasant trail that had been recently used by horses) that Heather referred to me as "Rick the perfect husband." I knew my part in the whole affair; I was far from that.

Boom, boom, boom.

Weekends were Erin's busiest times at the store so I could run for hours. I endured the self-imposed hardship of an unrelenting sun or thigh-deep snow happily bushwhacking through spring-loaded, eye-poking saplings if that was the direction Dave wanted to take us. We could not avoid the hills. In fact, we relished them. One summer, we punished ourselves on several occasions by scrambling up all nine runs at the ski club. Sweat washed away everyday fears about client satisfaction, money supply, or what life was all about. But never the Heavy Thing; it is insoluble still.

After long runs, I felt a little guilty for having a way to sequester Erin's depression. I operated in the misguided belief that in some similar way, the legion of loyal customers, the acclaim, the interviews on TV and in magazines of the clever personality behind the popular store were helping her. I returned from long runs, renewed and hungry. Saturday nights, in the middle of our fifteen acres, I fired up the patio BBQ while Erin prepared dinner in her award-winning house. Through the dining room window, I observed the choreographic laying of cutlery, the careful placement of wine glasses and candles as if the antique pine table was about to seat respected foreign dignitaries, which, in a way, the rest of us were. At rare times like these, the Heavy Thing would float away for a while.

Boom, boom, boom.

Maybe because I'm leaving, I can't run hard enough to slough off the sticky fear I didn't "do enough." The Heavy Thing used to be "what can be done for Erin?" It bullies me still.

"Do enough" is a finger stab to the chest, vague code for either culpability or ineptitude. I couldn't or wasn't able to recognize the truth of how bad Erin's condition was—first, to myself and eventually, to everyone else. I kept the wheels on the bus. I screwed it up. My greatest deficiency was the inability to understand that marriage and money couldn't undo Erin's mood disorder and, in fact, her illness was going to destroy both. I should have brought everything to a halt. I should have stopped the store that was losing so much money. I could have stepped in with a new physician, stopped the endless combinations of drugs that never worked—or made sure she kept taking them even when she reported she felt fine. I could have stopped working for a while and supervised a more rigorous regime of cognitive therapy. Instead, Erin stopped.

Knowing that depression, not her personality, was responsible for the listlessness and agitation and the source of every uncomfortable hour in her life wasn't much of an analgesic. The weight of the mood disorder crushed Erin as it kept me running. I resent it still but if that was pointless confession then, it's not even worth a footnote now.

The forest trail hurries from Belfountain to the river weaving decisively along the brow of the escarpment over pediform cedar roots and around white-daubed boulders, some as big as houses. At the quarter mark of the run I encounter the prone form of a fifty-foot black oak, ribbed with leafless branches. I can vault through the largest interval of them by thrusting my left arm like a pole vault and swing over but in winter it's prudent to mount the trunk springboard style, as I do now, left foot first, jumping onto it and then immediately pushing off, enabling me to hurry down the slope to the bridge over the river.

This dead tree, undiminished after seven years, is more securely fastened to the landscape than it ever was upright. It fell across the path during an ordinary winter night, which I resented at the time because running in snow is a continuous obstacle to running fast. No more building up for this tree, but I doubt anyone will come into these woods with a chainsaw to cart off ten-foot cords of firewood, so it's here forever. I'll be long gone before it transmutes into bark chips and mulch. This broken column—a former tree—definitely resident in the here and now but placed mysteriously in the living world for its useful contribution to regenerating soil (admittedly it's at a very early stage of decay) and for its random gift of acorns seeking purchase in the forest floor. On the eternal cycle, "big log" is not as dynamic a point as "seedling," "sapling" or "mature tree." It's time the tree dissolved. And so it will.

This place marks twenty minutes out from the cabin. If I'm ahead of or behind my best pace, it's here I make stride or breathing adjustments. I have the runner's habit of wanting to acquire a particular, personal rhythm on every occasion. Inside my head, a databank of runs contrasts this present surge to every past version of this experience. I've been on this trail and at this place many times before Erin died and this small piece of continuity offers provisional pleasure.

Boom, boom, boom.

I dial down my breathing and the trochaic beating on my brain softens. By the time I enter the provincial park, the beat will become a dull thud until it slips below the surface. It's then the run really begins.

It's magical thinking to believe I can possess this thread of land just by being on it. I used to imagine that living on fifteen acres conferred a kind of proof that I was getting ahead. By building my own house—not that *I* built any part of it, unless you include the coaxial wire my dad and I dragged through the stud walls on six consecutive wet autumn Sundays—I thought the experience and result should inoculate me against the stresses of work and provide happiness. I've lately thought, however, that if nothing can be owned, then why regret the loss of the house? Ironically, I won't even be able to rent the cabin when I get back—if I do come back; the owners have put it up for sale. I'm running out of options—and I can't help laughing at the pun.

A pair of screeching blue jays plummeting through emerald tendrils brings me back to the present. It is chilly under these cedar boughs; the sun kindles the foliage, which, in turn, perfumes the air. In the quiet pauses, I hear the cry of an osprey thirty feet above, and the surging Credit River thirty feet below. I cast my eyes on its rippling water, examine semi-visible seams and currents and imagine dawdling brown trout that wait for the river to deliver food. Out of sight, the osprey waits for the trout to make a slight motion, a pivot of maybe six inches.

The trout are deliberately lazy, intent on a single goal: survival. Spring will come when I am away and they will begin again the process of gaining weight, preserving energy so they can grow faster. Trout brains are the size of quarters and I suppose this ultimately is their greatest advantage. It must be invigorating and relaxing simultaneously not to be distracted by mortal threats, to think only about a goal, without ever realizing how deficiently such an arc of interest portrays the world. Or at least appetite-building. Trout eat anything nourishing: minnows, sculpins, crayfish—and fry, trout spawn less than five weeks old. They will eat their own progeny, nothing personal. Until he feels strong enough to locate and defend his territory, a trout keeps eating. A small space under a rocky ledge or in a pool, like one that I start to see through the trees just upstream from the railway trestle, might become home.

The trestle that spans the merging forks of the Credit River and the two sides of the gorge passes high above the road. The road links the village to the main highway six miles distant. On summer weekends, it riffles like water with gleaming Harleys and pristine suvs. There haven't been freight trains on this track for decades, but there's a vintage locomotive that hauls tourists from Orangeville to Brampton and back on weekends.

The trail abruptly leaves the woods at the bridge. Farther down the road, past the bridge are two trailheads, but if you haven't got a Bruce Trail map—and most tourists don't—you'd never know. Hikers assume the trestle and bridge at the forks of the Credit is the end of the line so they take a look at the waters cascading under the bridge then reverse themselves and return to the village certain they've seen it all.

Through the gauzy evergreens, I see sunlight catching the river surface but I will not see any fish. I do not have the skill to judge the submerged geography of the river for victims of a blue winged olive, hendrickson, or sulpher dun.

What I see is a cop, and his mouth is open wide enough to swallow a hooked fly.

I have never seen anyone on this trail in winter, much less a cop. I look past him, down the hairpin turn to the bridge. This is, as the sign proclaims, a scenic route, as bucolic as a postcard photo. But down there, under the railway trestle lies an arrangement of orange pylons like wizardly hardhats, a cat's cradle of yellow emergency tape, and a yellow truck topped off with a hydraulic crane not yet raised.

"You can't go any further," the cop says. His face twitches for air. He'd been ready to flag down cars from the village, not people on foot falling out of the woods. I'm surprised, too: why can't I continue maybe a hundred yards over the bridge to the park? The cop senses I need a reason to alter my course. He points where I want to go with a crooked finger. "The storm last night brought down the power line around there. You'll have to go back."

Back where? Like hell. I'm on a run.

He can't see the Heavy Thing, but still.

Get out of my way. You're on my land, officer. No trespassing.

"Look," I say. "What if I cross the river right here, to the other side and go past wherever the wire is. I'll pick up the road down there." I make a high, open-palmed gesture as if my proposed resumption is so benign we might as well be discussing the changing of a traffic light.

"Well, okay," he says, but I can tell he doesn't really understand my proposed re-routing. He's focused on cars. Cars won't be travelling this road for a while, that's clear. The power authority crew has only just hoisted a man in a cherry picker to the transformer box. Re-hooking the wire is going to take some time, more than I am willing to witness. Not being in a car is my only advantage but it won't last long.

"Well, okay," he says again and that's all I need. I scramble down the riverbank and jump commando-style into the water like Dave on one of his adventure races. It is cold. I lose the feeling in my feet and ankles immediately but it's only twenty or twenty-five feet wide so how long can the numbness last?

On the far side, I discover there is not nearly enough shoreline to manage walking so it's back into the river punctuated by stepping stones. This ridiculous detour carries on for several minutes more than I ever intended. Above I can hear a portable generator moaning and the crane ratchet but I'm still too low to see it. A couple of people are laughing. I take five or six exaggerated strides around where I figure the wire must be, splashing like a Navy SEAL, and then pull myself up the bank. I am about to say, "No harm done," and there it is—the wire, a black serpentine line. Not so fierce-looking. I am cold and wet standing before five thousand volts but what's the fuss? I have no desire to take my life; it's not about that. I'm also thinking how easy it must have been for Erin to just lean in a little closer to the railing. I realize with a chill what it is: she was being defiant, decisive. As if to say, "Take that. You think death's tough? I've suffered depression my whole life. Death's not so tough. This is my call. I get what I want—a way out of this tiresome chaos."

"Hey! What! Where did he come from?" another cop shouts, so frantic and loud that the sound seems disembodied. The outburst crackles like wood bursting in flame. Everything about its urgent tone—the short words, the indignation and worry in his voice—telegraphs a certainty that I do not realize the wire's immediate danger, or worse, that I do and I am preparing to ignore that and willingly touch it. And this assumption pisses me off. I don't need anyone to point out senseless tragedies. If I inadvertently touch that wire, his superiors will hold him responsible for his failure to properly supervise the site. But that's an unfair judgment. I wish I could shout back, "Relax, don't worry, I understand the kind of mess erecting itself in your brain and believe me, I'd never wish that on you." The cop's breath is steaming like a locomotive's, he's shuffling into a half-hearted motion, not sure if he can stop me before I take another step and probably wondering what he will do if he gets this far. It's possible he'll make for his vehicle but it is nearer to me than him and he hasn't figured out if I'll wait for his arrival. I am calculating, too, the icy snow surface, the distance to the trailhead. I decide I have no time for a lecture, especially as I cleared this little mistake with his colleague. I don't want to miss the plane. There is a trailhead around the bend in the road that will take me back to the cabin but I will have to sprint if I expect to outrun a car. The cop's just past his vehicle. I bolt and the cop gives up. It's all over but the shouting.

I wonder if he knows what I know: you cannot choose your own wounds. I run as fast as I can.

SAINT LUCIA

75¢ Lesser Antillean Pewee

"SOMETIMES I STOP, STUNNED
SUDDENLY TO DISCOVER
DAZZLING THINGS, THE
EXISTENCE OF WHICH
I NEVER SUSPECTED."

— CLAUDE MONET

Through the Unremembered Gate

A leaf, a small pebble, a ray of light...I savor a mysterious, delightful joy as I separate their imperceptible tones and their elusive reflections. And I realize that I had never really looked at anything. Ever. That's all to the good.... Sometimes I stop, stunned suddenly to discover dazzling things the existence of which I never suspected.

—Claude Monet

The most beautiful thing in the world is, of course, the world itself.

—Wallace Stevens

X MARKS THE SPOT—and it's the name of this room, the same room at Ladera in Saint Lucia where Erin and I came on holidays. Under a gnarly eucalyptus tree clutching my last Christmas present to Erin, this is where it's going to begin.

Because of this destination, I got a couple of squinting looks from friends, but I'm less worried about where to start this quest than what I should bring to it: three big paperbacks; maps of London, Singapore, Bali, Australia, and New Zealand; the drawing pen; my diary; a sketchbook. And the iPod that Erin never opened.

I have shut down the business for a while; months not weeks. I don't intend to spend all that time flat on my back but it's on the agenda for hours each day. To judge by the wiry appendages leading to my head, anyone observing me would think I was on life support, which is not so far from the truth.

I've wrapped the iPod in a beach towel to keep it dry. A wet wind is rinsing the leaves above my head. I am about as high or comfortable as you can get in Saint Lucia. But no one can see me. Through the tree, I have been staring at the Pitons, two volcanic peaks. Beside the mug, the diary sits like a ringing telephone, wanting some attention. But there is no telephone, no TV, and no e-mail. This morning it feels pointless to record any more thoughts. The prospect of writing can't compete with the view of two magnificent green peaks rising out of an azure sea. Inside my torpid body resides a hope that the sun and clouds will work out a compromise so I can stay hooked up to music and keep staring at the Pitons and stay dry. Maybe the combination of the music and the view will stop my chattering brain.

There is nothing between me and the outside world, not even a window or a handrail. My room has three walls; the deck pushes through where the fourth wall should be. Room X is perched in the very middle of the ridge that runs between the twin peaks. From it, I am able to survey the banana shapes of boats arriving after a night of fishing and the silver threads of yachts heading for Bequia or Martinique almost as well as the hawk looking for breakfast in the valley below. He may see more or glide as he pleases but I can remain in this hidden spot as long as I want.

I am experiencing music alphabetically.

"Allegro Moderato" from Beethoven's *Piano Concerto No.1* comes first, followed by Sarah Vaughan's "All of Me," Led Zeppelin's "All of My Love," and Keith Jarrett's "All the Things You Are." It will take some time to hear "Zing Zong," a mambo tune I don't remember programming. The sequence of unrelated kinds of music is fascinating; I have no idea what's next. Still my brain chats away. Why did she get her hair highlighted two days before she died?

I'm re-reading six-month-old entries in the diary as if it were a car-owner's manual and I hoped to come across some useful device I didn't know I had.

Some of what I'm unearthing is too brittle to handle safely. Did we love each other? I question the provenance of every memory. There's nothing to restore. I hope this archeology counts for something. Is that what a quest is: a dig of yourself?

It's harder to die, but at least it's a finite experience. Thinking about it goes on and on. It's also strange how hard it's been to convince some people that my wife continues to be dead. By telephone, mail, and e-mail, people seek payment for services Erin won't ever need again—hardly put off by her death. I sometimes feel they'd rather speak to Erin or someone in authority, that I am getting in the way; like the lighting wholesaler from Pennsylvania who'd taken Erin's order at the Atlanta gift show just weeks before she died.

"I know she'd want our products," the woman told me as if desk lamps were in demand in the afterlife.

I paid a penalty for "early termination" of her Explorer. The dealer was a wooden-faced individual and I inferred from his constant calls that he thought Erin was weaseling out of the lease. I sent a cheque to Erin's matrimonial lawyer on receipt of a letter that linked sympathy for my loss and a request for $247 in a single sentence. My matrimonial lawyer, though, well into our separation agreement when I called, was truly chilling when I told him the news. He didn't want any more money but his reaction was more intimidating than any other I'd heard. He said, "Wow. She really must have been depressed."

Most people like the waitress at breakfast this morning (who remembered Erin calling her "Queen Latifa" and thanked me for the CDs we'd given her), fumbled through "I'm sorry" and her eyes implored me to explain what happened. It's helpful to console others.

Last night I had the recurring nightmare: Erin has come back and wants to reconcile. Having it in Saint Lucia made it more vivid than usual and I said what I always say, "But you are dead." It's a protest. As if reconciliation was another one of her expensive spending binges during a manic episode that would only wear out both of us.

People always assume I had done the leaving, but Erin moved out one bitterly cold January night into the furnished apartment above her furniture store in the village. When she called to tell me our marriage was over, I was making dinner, two place settings. It was an abrupt anti-climax to a long manic stretch during which we'd managed to agree it was time to sell our house and close the store.

I immediately drove over, not expecting to retrieve her, but angry and certain this was the end. "What are you doing?" I said through the crack in the door but we both knew the entreaty was meaningless. She had been on the phone to someone. She held the receiver from the cord like the woman who had witched our well by dangling a crystal pendant. The door remained partially open. "Don't come in," Erin said, in case I was thinking about it. It was over like that. I stamped out my frustration on the stairs thinking I should call someone, but whom?

Unreasonably, I thought she'd be happier living by herself, maybe capable of becoming healthier. After that we met or talked once a week. She worked, if possible, even harder and managed to close the business with enough cash to retire almost all the store's debts. During that last phone call, two days before her death, I asked her how she was doing.

"Too many endings," Erin said.

It must be Sunday; I hear the bells in Soufrière or Choiseul. At Erin's memorial service, our minister—who favoured an earring and the hair colour of early Sting—carried on his unorthodoxy with a candle-lighting ritual she would have appreciated. Especially when the waxy overflow caught fire and everyone, even people standing at the back, laughed softly, as if it was a sacrilege.

Some days I'm glad we didn't divorce.

I have no idea what I am supposed to do next. If my task is to find peace of mind, the Voice has suggested, I'll be gone a long time. Since evicting business concerns from my mind, it's now impossible to avoid the empty space left behind. What will I fill it with?

I take up the pen and doodle sketches of the faithful diary, the iPod, the coffee cup, but my heart's not in it. Good diary. Sit. Roll over. Speak. And it does speak. Or something is speaking. It says:

Draw yourself out.

Somewhere I hear a rooster crow, and then nothing.

Several hours later I jolt upright, just in time to scoop up the iPod and save the sketchbook from certain drowning. I fasten my running shoes and grab a shirt. I have had a good route for several years that starts from the security hut under the enormous teak gate, carved as a superhuman arm with elongated fingers pointing to the western sky where the sun is still pearl white. Christopher the security guard hails me. I tell him this barrier is the long arm of the law, and he laughs.

"*Saka fete?*" (How's it going?) I ask.

"*Moi bien*, Mr. Clewes."

Perhaps the humidity will break long enough to deal with the steady climb to Belle Plain, past the farmers' co-op. If the sun reappears on the way down to Fond St. Jacques, I can slip into the shade of the broad-leaved immortelle trees that verge the broken road. And after I cross the meandering creek, the sun will be a dusky spotlight above the velvet curtained hills of Zenon.

People are becoming my landmarks.

"*Saka fete?*" I ask Wendell, who lives in the last house in Fond St. Jacques.

"*Moi bien*," he replies, not surprised to see me after a year.

Through the warped window frame of a ruined wood house, Wendell proffers a gurgling laugh and drops a grapefruit into my hands. The reading glasses exaggerate the size of his cocoa bean-dark eyes. He removes his cigarette briefly to smile and flash his gold teeth. He was in the Royal Navy. He has told me so every trip and this is the fifth time in Saint Lucia. I catch my breath, eat half the grapefruit and gulp from my water bottle. I hope his customary slow manner of speech will not delay me reaching Soufrière Cathedral before sundown. Wendell does remember where I am from but wants to know when I will be back and gives me a bittersweet bush orange. Goodbye, Wendell. Goodbye, Canada.

At the entrance to the rain forest, children giggle when they see my white legs and a few braver ones follow me like pilot fish. A pair of zebra-skinned mongrels cautiously challenges me. The tourists that come all the way from the capital city of Castries by open Land Rover, roaring through these nameless hamlets, are never investigated by mangy dogs as I am. It's a cruel technique but I learned a long time ago to discourage dogs by swiftly raising a clenched fist as if it held a rock.

The scent of pungent charcoaled chicken pulls at my nostrils. Roadside braziers are managed by young girls sitting cross-legged before them, gripping rolls of tin foil like scepters. The sweet aroma transports the genial chatter of men at dominoes in a rum shop, who slam their pieces defiantly, winning points or not. Half way, a tidy stucco rum shop comes into view. The story goes it's owned by a merchant sailor who married a woman from Copenhagen. Their kids, grown men now, speak Danish when information is worth keeping from customers.

I think grief is like a private code, a dead language I speak fluently but that no one else knows.

What was I thinking, wanting to revive Soufrière? Even in poverty, there is more richness and certainty in life here: children preparing chicken dinners, men who work in the banana plantations washing their naked bodies in the stream, cutlasses resting on neatly folded clothes. By unspoken agreement we do not acknowledge each other.

But I do acknowledge other runners on the road and have learned many things. An exchange teacher from Kyoto—who can't be five feet tall—challenges herself on the inclines and flows easily downhill. She explained that in exchange for building an over-engineered breakwater and docks in Choiseul, Japanese factory boats can legally fish inside the territorial limits of Saint Lucia. A Soufrière fireman who always runs in an Italian cycling outfit resplendent with European sponsorship badges advises against carrying water. Most often, I cross paths with a Creole businessman named Fatty who reformed his shape years ago but never lost the name. It was Fatty's French ancestors who settled Soufrière two centuries ago. His father owns anything worth owning: used car dealerships, hotels, import/export companies, building supplies. Except for the gold teeth, Fatty smiles just like Wendell.

Even Rosemary at the front desk wasn't sure where they were. I run my finger over the island's eleven *quartiers* like a surgeon who knows where to cut.

"Richard, we're going to have to call you 'Postman,' eh?"

Boguis, Marc Marc, Bexon, Fond Assor. So far, I've visited forty, maybe fifty "sub-postal stations," designated rooms in cement block and tin-roofed chattel homes on stones embellished with rusted enamel "Post Office" signs or a board painted in crude red and white calligraphy. Just as often, it is sign-less. Post offices exist so residents can pay their light and water bills. Occasionally, news comes from a daughter studying in Cuba, grandchildren in England, an auntie in St. Croix, a husband in Brooklyn, or a nephew in an army unit in Germany or Iraq. No one had ever seen a tourist cross the threshold of these post offices.

Nigel, the minivan driver (as distinct from Nigel the hotel chef) is busy all day ferrying tourists to the sulphur springs or to the beach and managing a reggae band at night but he's intrigued enough to want to drive me to my mythic places. He cannot understand why I collect cancellations of stamps especially in places with no appeal to tourists, or to Nigel for that matter. It started before, when lying by the hotel pool didn't appeal to me as it did to Erin. I never thought this collecting would one day become an idiosyncratic method of ensuring I pay attention to moments in time—and a glimpse into the lives of people I would never have otherwise known.

They are called postmistresses. To find them, I've learned to distrust ancient road signs and to not be discouraged by half-constructed buildings. Villages are a hodge-podge of history. The prosperous and the poor live side-by-side. Postmistresses are banana farmers, bakers, dry goods shopkeepers, tailors, sailors, mechanics, nurses, even organizers of illegal cock fights. In Banse, I sat in the shade of a miniature arena, built from tree limbs and cast-off wood watching two popular roosters grab and jump at each other like NFL linemen. On the windward side of the island we climbed dusty, crooked hills. There, we discovered the village of Americ, obscure even to Nigel. He said he couldn't understand the local accent. "They're *Americ*–ans, I guess," he said. There were other mysteries, too. We looked all over for "Odeon" and settled for "Aux Leon." I inspected the cancellation on the stamps, to be sure. It read: "Au Lyons." As far as I can tell there's not a single stamp collector among the postmistresses. But they all know me. "How's the madame?" the women want to know and I say, "Fine." The General Post Office (GPO) shut down Patience, Grace, and Mon Repos and with them, three small salaries. In Saltibus, I hailed Mrs. Virgin Montrose, who, with a smile suspended between pride and embarrassment, pointed out Voodoo prayers on scraps of paper tucked above every doorway—for protection from misadventures—and the GPO. In LaMaze, isolated by a mud slide that destroyed their road, I trekked into the post office. I asked grinning Yvette, the postmistress there, "Weren't you pregnant the last time I was here?" In Jacmel, Antoinette passed away unexpectedly. Her daughter took up her mother's duties. Everywhere, life goes on.

At the front desk, Rosemary makes arrangements for guided climbs of Petit Piton, the taller of the two. There is a tuft of green on the roof of its head. Where trees cannot root, the Piton's cranial bones are exposed to the sun. If I didn't know better, I couldn't imagine a way over its steep shoulders.

Driving to the trailhead, I pass young women and barefoot children balancing bamboo woven baskets of oranges, limes, guava fruit, and switches of basil. More prosperous farmers make the trip to Soufrière market on the jitney buses that rush past our Land Cruiser, horns complaining. The buses have names—*The Enforcer, No Problem, Jah Protect I and I*—painted above their windshields. A ride costs two dollars.

The Petit Piton trail starts in gritty, brown soil. The road to the trailhead carries on to the Hilton Beach Hotel gate where the Iranian owners barged in white sand from the Dutch Antilles but we stop well before that last, longest hill. The guide parks his truck in front of a dilapidated estate house that has the complexion of stained leather and we stumble out: me, a doctor from Columbus, South Carolina, and his wife. The government's home for seniors marks the trail's ingress. I wonder what old Lucians sitting on the barren verandah think of three tourists paying for five hours of hard, purposeless walking.

The soft footing quickly yields to a path embedded with small, sharp rocks, occasionally obstructed by mossy boulders or thick trees. Everywhere, low-hanging vines and waist-high grasses bite like teeth, as if the mountain was trying to swallow us. For the first two hours, I match the guide's pace. When we clear the treetops though, everything changes.

First, the path has become vertical, a rough-hewn ladder of flinty stone and contorted roots. There are pre-rigged ropes to assist us at every stage but I am amazed at my progressive weakness; I have no upper body strength left. The doctor tells his wife who is baulking at another narrow passage between two rocks, that there is no other way up and he's right but this diagnosis isn't helpful. Her delay makes clear how high we have come and for a long, uncomfortable moment, I consider what unthinkable things could happen.

Second, I can see fifty miles in three directions. Yachts on a broad reach from Rodney Bay appear to be sliding towards the Pitons. I can see the inexorable flow of jitney buses coursing like white cells through the coast road to Soufrière. To the south, meringue clouds fringe Saint Vincent. And there, just over the scrub trees, is my spot, Room X. It looks precarious from this vantage point, too close to the edge of things, an almost accidental accommodation by special agreement between man and nature. I can't look anymore. At this moment I'm flattening myself against the rock face unable to ignore the panorama and the dreadful sense of vertigo. We are nearly at the top but the guide says we must keep going. It should be simpler, I think, a little less dangerous. How to get down if up is so hard?

On the last stage, I tug as hard as I can, driven by a kind of resentment for the last four hours. At the top, there is immediate relief, a moment of calm and even brief merriment. With each breath, real or imaginary difficulties vanish. The adrenalin is pumping and the summit is charged with the air of eternal spring. We take turns passing the guide a camera, thanking him profusely, and generally acting like we'd conquered Everest. The sun feels good on our faces. A small wind combs the grasses and scrubby trees. I can see Room X very clearly. Erin is in the chaise lounge, reading a book, and smoking. I shout at the top of my lungs and flail my arms but she can't see me.

I am sitting dangling my feet in the plunge pool, just where Erin was two years ago. I look back up at the craggy balcony of Petit

Piton where the guide took me that day and where this morning, miniscule flecks of colour, today's climbers, move at the summit.

I am drawing the Pitons, but it's more like I have succumbed to them, as if someone else has taken my hand. At first it's mere doodling. I think, "If I'm going to be possessed, why can't it be by talent?" Then a hint of organization emerges; the pen nib goes here but not there. I recognize the shape of Gros Piton, its deep folds like a conic brain. It is playful, this drawing. With a little more focus, I can discern the liquid pattern of sunlight and shadow on the Piton's slopes as if the light and dark were creeping lava flows of paint, sticky and shiny. Then come unravelling lines, thin and thick, emulating the crescent tops of the breadfruit and mahoe trees. I see for the first time how complex and deeply textured the trees make the Pitons. With no trouble at all, I am able to pick out the sharp flourish of a single palm out of hundreds, then allow my eyes to fly in figure eights above the Pitons so they can inspect the curve of the emerald peaks and sparkling sea. This way of seeing, the manner of drawing—I feel as though I've come back to a place I evacuated long ago.

In the afternoon the burgeoning clouds have wispy tails; they blow through the Pitons like ghosts too busy to haunt.

The Rastafarian Tennis Pro

The days are stacked against what we think we are: it is nearly
impossible to surprise ourselves.
                    —Jim Harrison, *The Theory & Practice of Rivers*

I AM CRUSHING the ball that Vernon lobs.

Being so close to the equator in January, there's no soothing
dusk surrounding the Hilton Jalousie courts, just the tail end of a
ferocious heat. At 6 PM, a coveted time for lessons, I am playing
against Vernon Lewis, the hotel pro, although the only conflict of
which I am aware is between me and the sun. Brain-broiling rays
mock my hat, coming from impossible angles. The sun itself will
signal the end of my hour digging up Vernon's balls, by slipping
hard into the Caribbean Sea, as fast as barbells discarded by an
Olympic weightlifter. Weightlifting approximates how it feels to
pull my fifty-year-old body around this tidy green grid.

This is some kind of fun.

At least it was supposed to be. This is the first planned event
on my self-help tour. If fetching tennis balls off the racquet of a

three-time Davis Cup section champion isn't a visitor attraction yet, watching tourists self-flagellate in tropical heat might become one. Depends how much worse it gets out here. January is probably cooler than July. Vernon could try harder but I doubt he will. This is his last tennis match of the day and my first in probably ten years.

We volley.

Vernon constantly smiles as if remembering a funny story, too long to explain. He moves like a blade of grass in the wind. His dreadlocks sway like jump ropes. Only in competition, I learn later, will Vernon bind his dreads into a ponytail. He is a Rastafarian, finding Jah after ascending to the competitive heights of regional tennis; he was world famous across the Caribbean for more than a decade. Then he returned to his mother's house beside the Catholic church in Choiseul. Tired and no longer interested in trophies or prize money, he almost gave up tennis forever but for the re-discovery of his faith in a power beyond his control. People who knew the shy, slightly-built kid who never lost a match between Port-of-Spain and Miami tell me that Vernon at thirty—old age in tennis—is even better since retiring.

We volley without a break for several minutes, ignoring my out-of-bound shots. His modesty is infuriating.

The heat is driving me to hit the ball with greater force. Soon my eyeglasses are lacquered with sweat, which makes judging the ball's trajectory even more challenging. His presence through my lenses may be distorted but I can hear Vernon quite clearly. I am aware of my own breathing, too. I am exhaling through my mouth as if the court was a vast dining room table and I had to blow out the candles of a birthday cake, over and over again.

Of the two, I prefer listening to Vernon's soundtrack to my own. He is grunting in time to the ball, not to emphasize the effort behind his graceful and precisely executed ground strokes—and certainly not to intimidate me—but as a sympathetic, almost reverential response. He grunts as poetically as jazz pianist Keith Jarrett laments, sighs or moans. Both men look to be in awe of their respective activity, as if something else was at work. Vernon's quirky sonic reflex accompanies every return; he is being carried away by his own music.

The compressed tennis ball makes a hollow and hypnotic sound, like the back beat to the Fine Young Cannibals' "She Drives Me Crazy." Vernon isn't apparently aware of his profound connection to the melody of our game, but he's a full beat ahead of me, like an orchestral conductor, leading and waiting at the same time. I can see by his elastic stance that Vernon knows where the ball's going to go next. The ball behaves like a friendly dog hovering briefly before a stranger then returning to its owner, full of anticipation for requited love.

Meanwhile, I struggle to lengthen my back swing to more closely resemble my teacher's example but this is difficult because emulating Vernon's actions depends on how often I can surreptitiously mop my glasses. I want to avoid looking bad, which is a stupid motive. For one thing, I can't compete with Vernon. For another, I am pounding the ball as hard as I can. Shallow ambition diverts attention from my hot, sopping head.

I long to hear the music that carries Vernon away. Instead, my father's admonishment about important Saturday chores is lodged in my ears. "Don't get carried away," he used to say as if enthusiasm threatened the completion of our Saturday chores. "Focus on the job," he advised my brothers and me as we dug trenches exactly so many feet deep for cedar hedges or septic tanks or other useful purposes.

I need to let go. But leaving the mind unattended so I can re-experience life is a skill apparently beyond my grasp. I am off the work-debt-marriage leash, looking for other ways to rein in my freedom. I accept that I am on a quest of some kind. But even in the throes of a self-indulgent tennis lesson I can't screen out thoughts of Erin's suicide, the loss of the house, and lack of interest in working in advertising again any more than I can stop my glasses from sliding down my nose. I'm trying too hard. I keep thinking that not knowing what to do is bad and represents a kind of assault on my integrity. Or survivability.

I signal Vernon for a break. It's almost dark anyway. At the net, Vernon is grinning and complimentary. "You're hitting the ball hard. That's good, Richard. Can I offer a piece of advice?" Of course, I say, please. I mean, this is a tennis lesson. He swings his racquet in easy arcs, shifting from side to side in his spotless shoes tracing a kind of dance step.

"Sometimes you have to ask yourself: 'How hard do I have to hit this ball to get it over to the net?'"

Help me.

" TO ME THE MOST IMPORTANT THING
IS A SENSE OF GOING ON.
    YOU KNOW HOW BEAUTIFUL THINGS
ARE WHEN YOU'RE TRAVELING. "
    —— EDWARD HOPPER

An Unexpected Turn of Events

Be islands unto yourselves, seeking no external refuge.

—Buddha

IT WAS JUST ANOTHER DAY in paradise, the Wednesday before I left Saint Lucia. Beneath a serenely blue sky, departing tourists aboard a British Airways Boeing 777 were relinquishing a tropical island and deeply regretting it. At the precise and unwelcome moment when your consciousness re-constitutes details of what you left behind—work, relationships, the location of your house keys—you know the vacation is over.

Happily, I was several miles away, still in the thrall of the Pitons, scribbling and drawing, not scheduled to leave for another two days. Besides, my flight on Virgin Atlantic to London was just another segment, a link in a long chain, not the Dreaded Return Flight. The sight of windsurfers like runaway sails freely carving through the Caribbean Sea five hundred feet from buckled-down seats might stir a wish to restart a weeklong vacation but more likely each passenger was shifting from carefree sentience to the unequivocal mental alertness associated with ordinary, post-holiday life. They might almost expect an onboard announcement like: "Please make sure your brain is in the fully-upright position."

They didn't expect the British Airways captain to slowly taxi their aircraft right off the end of the runway.

What were the odds? The pilot overshot the runway turn-around point by a mere three feet. Immediately, the nose wheel became mired in the sandy turf. Doubtless, the pilot was surprised by this turn of events. For all the mobility his new location offered him, the captain might as well have parked in the middle of the cow pasture that surrounds three sides of Hewanorra Airport. Beyond the superb view the cockpit offers of "a horned island with deep green harbours," as poet Derek Walcott calls his home, the repercussions of a displaced plane far from its home started to sink in. Since no trucks on the island are capable of towing anything greater than a fully-loaded Buick, the plane would stay put for the time being. If possible, fuel would be pumped out to lighten the load. Luggage, mail, cargo—all of it had to come off. Along with passengers, of course. They were escorted—probably happily—back to a local hotel. While in London, some British Airways engineer—probably unhappily—picked up the phone in the middle of the night and heard a frantic voice beg for help.

For two days Saint Lucia was as remote as Antarctica. A taxi driver, sniffing for business around the front desk at Ladera, told me nothing could land or take off, since there is only one runway in Vieux Fort. The drama of the plane in the cow pasture played out in headlines for three days and replaced the island's preoccupation with the muddy progress of new Irish-built main highways being constructed to improve access to the airport.

What surprised me was the sense of isolation the grounding raised in me and the unappealing idea that I couldn't control my itinerary. I hadn't expected to be so susceptible to such a minor inconvenience. Of all the people visiting the island, I had the least claim for needing to get home. To be reunited with my new life, whatever or wherever it might be, was months from here. And yet, I didn't want to stay any longer on Saint Lucia. First my luggage bounced all over the West Indies before getting here a week late, now I can't get on a plane.

I wasn't accepting the unforeseen very well because, frankly, I'd had a vivid, life-altering sample of the unexpected and thought I had earned a few exemptions; an upgrade based on my Frequent Griever Points. The grounded plane was screwing with my trip, the only thing in my life I was interested in controlling. Truth is, no matter where you go, there you are.

And if I wasn't quite certain what my quest was all about, at least I knew much depended on hurdles placed in my path. A stuck plane didn't seem to fit the sequence of arriving, experiencing and departing. I asked Rosemary at the front desk if I might be able to stay for a few more days. She said it wouldn't be necessary since the situation at the airport would fix itself before my departure. She was right, of course.

Conveniently, engineers managed to safely tug six hundred thousand pounds of tourism revenue back onto solid ground just a few hours before my scheduled departure on Virgin Atlantic 032. We took off for the Atlantic as if our captain believed errant driving was contagious.

I peered at the dusk-lit scene below of re-boarding British Airways passengers, and wondered what the price tag for what I saw would be. I tested my vodka tonic with a sip and clinked glasses with my latest seatmate, a handsome fifty-five-year-old woman with perfect hair and a reserve suited to our section: first class.

I described the massive response to work the problem—equipment and crew that had to be scrambled, 150 hotel rooms for three hundred unexpected guests—and the massive costs. I suggested other airlines whose flights had been scrubbed—or worse, re-directed to nearby islands in mid-flight—would come up with their own bills for British Airways to pay.

I kept looking down on the tarmac until I could no longer make out the plane. The island shrunk from view. There was no sign of the economic disaster that had just occurred. At great cost, it was ready to go again; the plane hadn't sustained the slightest damage. Everything looked absolutely normal. And that, I realized, was what made the whole episode so strange. Including my anxiety about missing out on a stage of the quest which, I now realized, I hadn't.

I didn't share my insight with 12B. It would have made an awkward segue to my mildly received story about the ill-fated plane—and you do think about avoiding extemporaneous remarks on long flights. She smiled sweetly and asked if I'd ever been to Wiltshire. Like most tourists, she had a limited interest in the events of a holiday place now firmly tucked in the Pleasant Vacations cranial file, but I appreciated her conversational attentiveness. I said something like, "Isn't Stonehenge in Wiltshire but I bet you've never visited it," and I was right. We sustained an aimless, amiable chit-chat through a very good lamb shank to lights-out and seats-back without once revealing who we were or where we were going

" IT IS TO BE A SILENT SPECTATOR
OF THE MIGHTY SCENE ... BUT
NOT TO FEEL THE SLIGHTEST
INCLINATION TO MEDDLE
WITH IT. "

— WILLIAM HAZLITT

On Stolid Ground

I do not know whether there are gods, but there ought to be.

—Diogenes (412–323 BC)

IN THE PRE-DAWN DRIZZLE of Gatwick dozens of aircraft mainte-
nance vehicles were ducking under the wings of airliners I'd
never heard of, representing countries I couldn't locate on my
mental map of far-flung countries. After going AWOL on the first
leg of my trip, it was easy to imagine my only bag embarking on
an irretrievable trip to Gabon, Azerbaijan or some place (or airline) called Belavia.

At no other point during the travel experience is there a
greater sense that something's about to happen than when you
land or take off: the Beatles disembarking at Idlewild; Nixon's
sayonara from Marine One on the White House lawn; every NASA
mission shooting up a gantry. My coming-and-going is hardly
the stuff of history, but my being in London is irreversible.
The *Times* of London says: "UK Next Leg in Widower's Walk
Around Himself."

Here I am.

Headlines endure because nobody has time to read the full story. I crave the meaning of Erin's event, but I don't want to think about depression or suicide anymore. What's the point of going over it again and again? I want to know what happens next, but I'm no better than a stray topic sentence. I am the stranger riding into town that nobody finds strange. "Widower" doesn't nearly describe the former or evolving versions of me.

If it were just a matter of being widowed, or if we'd separated because we truly fell out of love, I could figure out a way to move on. But this is complicated. Erin's departure tugs at me, at everything I do, even my getaway. I am in limbo.

What I lack is mobility, which is ironic, given my clearly indicated round-the-world itinerary. And considering the futile years of acting decisively, adjusting moods with combinations of money or optimism while trying not to get caught under the wheels of Erin's mania and lethargy, it's a surprise to realize life's not going anywhere. I need to move, I want to move, but nothing moves. Time for me has been arrested. As if an unseen hand has driven a wedge between the hours of the day and between cause and effect of Erin's suicide, too. I didn't *do* anything in Saint Lucia. Still, the restitution of my drawing abilities proves, if nothing else, that sometimes nothing's better than doing nothing.

Maybe limbo is supposed to be good for the soul, or mine at least. My fellow passengers, despite being up in the air long enough to get used to it, are repelled by inactivity. They are more than willing to calibrate arms for the overhead compartments and one-handed dialing of cell phones rather than wait for the gangway. Frantic Blackberry retrievals are underway in all rows. For not one second longer than necessary do people consent to be between points A and B. I used to be an aisle seat, one row behind the bulkhead. Now I'm competing with the handicapped passengers for last one out.

In the interval, I imagine a creative opportunity for an airline (probably from Asia) looking to better the fully-reclining beds, an unrestrained video library in six languages, dangerously hot towels—all the aero lingo—and claim a competitive proposition of new and transcendent benefit: We'll Move Your Soul™. Or: It's not an Airbus; it's the Soul Train™.

Limbo just needs to be re-positioned as a valuable segment in life's journey. It's a state of mind, potentially the tourist equivalent of California or Florida, but more exotic and spiritually spare, like Tibet—without the remoteness and nasty weather, of course. Come to think of it, what more appropriate expression of the concept that nothingness is its own reward, than a nation without sovereignty?

No more awkwardness with China. Who needs land? Limbo adherents will be above material concerns, "soul-moving" between major US cities through its hub in Sedona. Air Limbo can finally put Tibet on the map after years of fruitless lobbying by Hollywood Buddhists. Air Limbo. Which means Richard Gere and Uma Thurman can do the pro bono TV spot. I will write a thirty-second script that casts them as Air Limbo flight crew, moving guru-like down the aisles of an extraordinarily beautiful aircraft, which would be either all white or transparent—even better. They will strap the passengers in just below the navel chakra and make suggestions about breathing technique.

"Let your thoughts pour over you like a waterfall. Don't try to stop them. Meditation isn't positive thinking, Mr. Clewes, or can I call you Richard?" says Uma.

Of course she can. They may be stars on a spiritual quest, but they put their mantras on one leg at a time, just like the rest of us. We're all Buddhists on this plane, right?

And what sound does limbo make? Something *om*-able; it has to be familiar but unheard of. Juxtaposition is everything. *Big Prayer Wheel Keep on Turning.* Or Yanni could re-arrange the Beach Boys' "I Get Around." What bliss. To spend hours and hours passing through clouds or empty skies with nothing to distract you but the soothing vocal texture of the Dalai Lama: "Ladies and gentlemen, this is your captain chanting."

I can't be the only traveller in life who wants to get past the destinations. I feel like a passenger in that joke, the one in the plane that crashes on the border between two countries. "Where should the survivors be buried?" goes the punch line. I don't know what is more disturbing: my decade of depression-defying acts of high-wire finance or the realization now, at this moment in London, that I never had a net.

Still, just about anything is better than being in the middle of a war with depression. Forget that the enemy infiltrated her personality so completely that neither one of us recognized her. Forget that there were times when I could not rouse myself into battle with it. Forget most of all, it wouldn't have mattered how much I'd loved Erin, it was never about that. The bad guys won. But at least after most skirmishes, the medics are allowed onto the battlefield to collect the dead and wounded.

Through the oval aperture of 12A, I watch the descent of wooden crates, mail bags, steel containers, battered suitcases, and more than a few examples of indigenously Caribbean lug-gage: the refrigerator-sized cardboard box, cinched tight and seconds away from splitting its sutures. As long as my bag remains incognito there is hope for our reunion. Meanwhile, the extractions from the underbelly of our plane are being force fed into long links of flatbeds. Despite their drab appearance, the miniature trains gallop towards the customs shed in rapturous choreography like animals in a three-ring circus.

Now I am standing outside, done with HM Customs and Immigration and my bag is obediently by my side. I climb into the front seat of a minivan with an inexorable craving for thick buttered toast and bacon. The heavy-set Pakistani driver follows the sun rising in the greasy eastern sky like a yolk about to sizzle. Down the road a few miles he obligingly pulls into a McPetrol café that offers a deeply satisfying variant of egg and muffin, and not-bad coffee.

What thoughts travel doesn't tame, coffee drowns.

It is a kind of progress to have made a journey across the vastness separating a green dot of an island where towing an airplane was a national concern, and the sprawling wealth of a first-world capital, once the imperial master of many Saint Lucias. Seven and a half hours in embarrassing comfort has nullified a gap that explorers, colonizers, slaves, and warriors risked their lives to cross.

The entire history and geography of the Atlantic Ocean were less of an impediment than I would have faced had my passport bar code not scanned. But I'm rolling along on the northbound London-Brighton road with commuters where Victorians once journeyed to the seashore to restore themselves after a long day of empire building.

I'm a meek participant in a conversation with the driver, Mr. Khan, whose grasp of the points of interest in London is limited to places clients have visited. I am keeping an eye out for the elusive Soho Square, which we thought we'd found a few times but we're sure will re-appear just around the corner. We have been talking about religion and politics with the cordiality reserved for strangers thrust together determined not to clash. The world may be a global village, but the villagers never leave the neighbourhood. He hates George W., but he's not sure why. We're crossing the Thames at Battersea, now famous for Whistler's *Old Battersea Bridge*, but I think that bridge is long gone like most of my university education. And somewhere around here is the "Dogs Home," where all London's strays have been welcomed for 160 years.

Now we are near the British Museum in Bloomsbury. We overshot Soho Square and the navigationally diffident Mr. Khan is having a tricky time with the one-way streets. On Great Russell Road we slowed down in front of the museum. I'm sure I could walk to the hotel from here if I knew where it was. But there's no rush, the coffee's warmish. And then I see the grand façade, the portico, and the pebble-carpeted grounds. I studied these columns in first-year university; Ionic, I'm sure. There are two rows of eight supporting the roof. The classic frieze above depicts men and women in drapery representing Drama, Poetry, Music, Mathematics, and Philosophy. This is *The Progress of the Human Race*. I remember that. The Victorians saw themselves as the new Greeks, having earned their virtues and this building was meant to leave no doubt. The British Museum was the vigorous centre of nineteenth-century scientific, artistic, and political worlds—Egyptian treasures wrestled away from Napoleon, the Elgin Marbles from Greece. In there, Karl Marx brought his lunch each day and wrote a best-seller called *Das Kapital*. This must be why the Socialist Bookstore is located right across from the BM front gate.

Under the goey canopy of metropolitan London, Saint Lucia's Pitons are melting into apartment and office blocks; glass and steel are expropriating volcanic cones that rose from the

Earth's core ten thousand years ago. Time is catching up with me again.

Presently, Mr. Khan figures out legal access to Frith Street, the cross-fade of my last destination and new one is complete.

The jet lag is starting to assert itself. As I lay on the bed in Hazlitt's Hotel, my thoughts careen through many topics but, as always, settle on mortality. Examining the bedside clock's alarm buttons takes all my energy. The display reads 8:30 PM, which is either wrong or I have lost a whole day. Either outcome suits me. I fall asleep.

I dream of a Pakistan International Airlines 747 that hovers and rotates above an enormous crane that now I see is a gigantic water gun. I am in a dockyard area of a city I don't know. The plane twists its wings into the cooling stream as benignly as an elephant might flip its ears. As I look, the aircraft's pitch and yaw quicken. People around me pass swiftly in cars or on foot and point up to emphasize the danger. To me, it is a mesmerizing display of aeronautics and not something deeply disturbing. I stay rooted to my spot, convinced that the complex control of the 747 that prevents it from dropping out of the sky will keep me safe from harm. But then it suddenly spins into a whirl that my eyes can't follow.

Then, at a much lower elevation, a little plane approaches heading directly for me, *North by Northwest*–style. But at the last possible second, when impact seems certain, this little plane banks out of my way. I have an impression that this too is a warning and if the pilot so decided, he—or she—could have killed me. All this activity and I am still unable to move. Now onlookers noisily complain about the reckless pilot but I return my attention to where the 747 had been spinning. There is nothing there. The sky is an empty canvas.

I am here utterly. There is no going back. What will happen, now that I know that much? I am afraid. Is there a moment of truth, the point at which everything in life that is meaningful—if that's the word—meets your total acquired humanness? That would be an attractive idea. It would have to be true for all of us. I think about that. And what I would do.

Come out, come out wherever you are.

66 ORIGINALITY is FEELING
the GROUND SUFFICIENTLY UNDER
ONE'S FEET TO BE ABLE TO
GO ALONE. 99

—WILLIAM HAZLITT

Walking for Godot

They say that time changes things, but you actually have to change them yourself.

—Andy Warhol

I BLINK.

The sun is up and, I'm guessing, it has been for a while. I hear scuffling on concrete, the indistinct gabble of overlapping voices. It must be Monday; the clopping feet are too fast to be tourists'. I am submerged in a bed with so much quilting I could be in a coffin. Two days later and I'm still jet-lagged. I feel like death. Appropriately, this room at Hazlitt's Hotel, the kind of place better suited to romantic weekends than a personal fact-finding mission, is in the basement.

Under my breath for the umpteenth time: "Erin would have loved this place. We never got to Europe."

What a shame that she will never see it.

But why should that matter? We're entitled to our own regrets at least. Europe probably doesn't hold a candle to the afterlife. That's a strange idea. Maybe I'm evading something. I should focus on more immediate concerns.

Why are you here?

I don't mean on Earth. I don't mean London. London's a pivot; a way to connect Saint Lucia to Singapore. Rather, what am I doing here, on this trip?

You are in pursuit of yourself.

That's the short answer. So far I've been able to stay one step ahead of the pursuer. My mind is vigilant, knows it's being hunted down by a patrol that couldn't care less whether or not I am receptive.

I picked this hotel on a whim. I just liked the name. I imagined it had something to do with a noble family or a famous hotelier. It is neither. Forty-eight Frith Street once belonged to an eccentric, now all but forgotten, nineteenth-century writer, William Hazlitt.

Eduarda at the front desk told me advertising people like to stay here because it's close to Soho's film edit suites and recording studios but at the moment there are no ad types. Unless you count me. Maybe I'm no longer a part of advertising's precocious achievements.

Like knowing all the hip hotels?

I'll ignore that. Did I fill in "profession" on the registration card? I can't remember. I can't be awake. I squint at a well-kerned page of the hotel brochure from the bedside. You have to admire the elegant, sensible, confident way the English render the printed word. The Garamond font informs me that Hazlitt rented rooms to stave off bankruptcy. He died at fifty-two, my age, "poverty stricken."

So much for that strategy.

Hazlitt's housekeeper thoughtfully stowed his body under a bed for a few days, until paying guests checked out.

Is this his room?

If I add up the time I've spent talking to myself it's probably a dead heat: me alone versus me in conversation with a revolving cast of cab drivers, front desk clerks, flight attendants, and customs officers. Typically, these people come from places other than where we meet. I'd like not to keep the world at arm's length all the time, but at the end of my arm there's this sketchbook and pen secured, duct-tape tight. It's part shield and weapon, part sword and stone. I yank the pen from its scabbard and an impulse to fence with what's around me takes over. An ordinary meal has become, by twists and turns, an exotic occupation of paper. I can't help myself. Drawing is not the equal of London, but it is more satisfying than any tourist site or conversation I have yet experienced.

I feel conspicuous. Not because I am a drawing automaton in planes, cafés and cabs, but because I'm certain I can't talk about anything other than Erin, that I will slip into a pathetic retelling of my recent life to a total stranger.

How far back into the sordid mess do you want to go, sir/madam? I've got all day, all trip, in fact.

I feel wide open, as willing to divulge the pent-up contents of my life as a river breaching a dam. Other times, I imagine my marital history as a graphic novel tattooed on every inch of my skin.

As we handed over our dinner trays, the Virgin Atlantic flight attendant asked me if I was an artist. In Saint Lucia, I filled three sketchbooks and showed her one. It is a reasonable question but No, thanks for asking—this is just a hobby. She thinned her eyes at my explanation; she'd watched me drawing all flight. Mildred had never before seen a passenger drawing their entrée and neither, apparently, had the captain. These days, I guess the pilot must be informed about any unusual activity among passengers without laptops. I gave her *Thirty-thousand-feet Dinner* and *Thirty-thousand-feet Breakfast*.

Drawing food is a narrow definition of a quest but it has a practical aspect; it enables me to eat alone. In fact, only during dinner do I ever realize I am alone. I think about the eccentric Renaissance paintings based on cleverly arranged eggplants and cherry tomatoes to make jolly portraits of Italian nobles, but this is different. I have decided to call my new art movement "Platescapes."

I have also been sketching semi-possible versions of the future in my head, but the contemplation is getting me nowhere. Action is what I have always been more comfortable with: the come-from-behind-win of an advertising account, marathons, bipolar spouses. I could quit work and become a full-time Platescapist, I guess. Or I could open an authentic local bar for tourists in Soufrière, a concept the two Nigels suggested. This would keep me out of the airport caricaturist game and a vast assortment of other dangerous job listings in Margaritaville. I could just keep drawing and eating until the money or the ink dries up. Innate knowledge might spontaneously enter the ink chamber of my drawing pen, impelling a boldly stroked annunciation about the Heavy Thing or quests in general. On the other hand maybe nothing's going to happen. In *Lawrence of Arabia*, Peter O'Toole emerges against all odds from the desert with the given-up-for-lost man. He throws pure defiance back at Omar Sharif: "Nothing is written," he says.

Nothing is written. Unless you write it.

The truth is, rescuing oneself—if that's what I'm doing—is a tedious, spasmodic, and occasionally middle-of-the-night scary business. It's nothing like the tension and relief of a big-screen conflict. The conflict is intransigent because—so far at least—I can't locate its source. Erin's not the culprit; she's the inciting incident. What wakes me up at night is the certain belief that I knew what I was doing when I married her. With exquisite precision, I picked a mate whose suffering from a debilitating mood disorder never seemed to impress my cognitive apparatus. I acted as if I believed love could cure depression, or worse, that I was doing something noble. That's one secret that needs no map to find. Perhaps that is an oversimplification, but let's start there. I won't get to the real secret—whatever it turns out to be—unless I can deal with my first hurdle: me.

I understand why friends—even strangers—hum along with the "I-feel-guilty" line I spout. It's a good tune that no one can get out of their heads and it comforts us all. But it's appeasement, a delaying tactic. I'm not guilty. The suicide's not my fault, but it hardly makes me feel better for saying so. And it sounds worse out loud. I should look squarely at the locus of my own crisis. Or maybe I'll lie here all day. This is my trip, why not? Do I have to be diligent every waking minute? Drawing and writing little, tiny thoughts in my diary? Maybe I can doze in every country I go. And after, I'll come up with a witty book, describing what I will come to know well, namely the things that can be done in bed apart from sex or sleep. I must do this before Bill Bryson does.

There is nothing in sight to encourage either option. To my immediate left is a small desk littered with last night's steak *frites* (good for two sketches) and a chair so nominal only someone under five feet would attempt to sit in it but a perfect cove for my pocket's paraphernalia: camera, keys, cash, map. To the far right, the BBC presents the latest information on floods in Wales. Wedged between the two is my very own sub-grade window.

Through it, I see the parade of disembodied shoes, the source of my unofficial wake-up call.

Must. Get. Out. Of. Bed.

I have a lukewarm urge to fall in step with the rest of humanity, which is a pretty pedestrian *satori*—if what I'm hearing fits the ISO standards for Zen Buddhist epiphanies. Londoners are making the pilgrimage to work.

Hit the road like Saul, come back as Paul.

Maybe this is not the ideal motivator. I am not religious, but I could go for a good, old-fashioned pilgrimage right about now. Mecca, Lourdes or Mount Fuji (which I hear has a well-lit path and provides guides twenty-four hours a day). With a pilgrimage you know what you're getting into. And more importantly—this is key—you know exactly when the quest is accomplished; as soon as you reach the end, it's done. If mine is about finding me, would somebody answer this: How will I know when my quest's done? Self-awareness of self-awareness? This is some kind of quest.

A neighbour's sister Nicky, a freelance ecology writer and an atheist, walked the Pilgrims' Route. It spans four hundred miles from the French side of the Pyrenees to Santiago de Campostella (during the Middle Ages they called it *Tierra Finis*, the end of the Earth). I asked her, "If you're not Catholic anymore, and it's not for spiritual renewal, why do it?"

"It's a good walk."

But now I am well out of bed, showered and shaved and moving around the room, a rotten night's sleep falling off me like a rocket gantry. I'm not exactly organized but Nicky's right: there's nothing like a walk to convince yourself that you are going somewhere. Especially when you're lost.

Upstairs, determined to receive from Eduarda some spiritual marching orders, I enter the atmosphere of the hotel's tiny reception area, rendered in a rich *sfumato* style. The January sun meekly penetrates ancient windowpanes facing Frith Street and daubs a new carpet (made to look antique) with delicate honey smudges. The glass is uneven and lumpy, pulled by gravity for 160 years. The concierge is draped in shadowy burnt sienna. She is a young woman from Lisbon. Hair, the colour of fortified wine, swirls to her waist. Being modern and resourceful, Eduarda will react unflinchingly to my soul enquiry.

What's the best thing to do in London for a week if your wife commits suicide, but your marriage was going down the tubes anyway and you're not sure what to do next?

Perhaps it can be rephrased slightly. I could focus on Hazlitt; maybe take a walking tour of his 1830 haunts? A new ghost would be nice.

Eduarda studies me, hunched witchlike, although she may be the only witch ever to wear Dolce & Gabbana. For her first trick, she changes some money and conjures a map of Soho with obscure historical annotations (the house where the world's first TV signal was transmitted; Ronnie Scott's jazz club where Eric Clapton learned to play guitar).

Then I ask her to invoke Hazlitt. Eduarda smiles broadly and apologizes. She knows "only a little about the great man." She means it ironically. But on this she is unmistakably sincere: "Hazlitt committed career suicide."

And this: "He loved badly."

This gets my attention. With a second, slow smile, Eduarda the Elegant Witch hands me my map and withdraws to her leather perch below the check-in counter, disappearing in the smoky air. I think discovering the gory details of Hazlitt's demise, and why he ended up worse than I, will be a cheering experience. This is surely a livelier alternative to wrestling down to the ground weighty issues like life and death, God and salvation, loneliness, or loss of faith, which—as any self-respecting existentialist will tell you—is technically impossible so long as you remain in a basement hotel room.

I will be walking not waiting for Godot. I might even bump into him.

66 HE WAS NOT AWARE OF it
BUT THE WORLD WAS BEGINNING
to PRESS AROUND. THE
PEN of the WANDERING JOURNALIST
HAD DONE THE TRICK. 99
~ R.K. NARAYAN

Living and dying

Still Life

> It should be being home, being home. It is not.
> It is being outside of the outside, outside
> Of the very outside without which an inside
> Cannot be. This is why we send postcards
> —Wallace Stevens, "A Postcard from Paris"

THERE'S A LOT THAT is over my head.

I'm half-way through a museum tripleheader. I tilt my head to imagine the additional height of a gentleman's top hat. This gap, my taxi driver Claude announces through the speakers, has determined the vertical dimension of London cabs for a hundred years. A gentleman must safely enter, sit, and alight from a cab without disturbing his hat.

"Why do you go to museums?" he asks. Fair question.

A year ago I could not have imagined myself inside a museum much less spending whole days at the Tate Modern, National Portrait Gallery, and the British Museum. As to why the interest in art resurfaced in Saint Lucia after thirty-odd years, I'm in the dark and as uninformed as why cabs in 2004 are still built to a charming, irrelevant nineteenth-century standard.

Charming but irrelevant—that summed up my attitude to art as freshly-minted junior art director in an ad agency twenty years ago. Directing art; it sounds comical now. What moved my eyes to see again that the world is a living work of art: the Pitons or a deeply buried memory of a lovely Monet? I'm dying to introduce Claude the Cabbie to Claude the Impressionist, but I can't get a word in edgewise.

My driver is giving a cockney perspective on the evilness of Tony Blair and the greatness of the West Ham football club. A few times I have made affirmative noises and nod, usually when I think he's drawing fresh breath. From the passing landscape, he roots out a date for a church, building or bridge—the usual landmarks—and one he calls the Gherkin. From the crackling speaker on my side of the glass partition streams his literary commentary, too. Dickens, Shakespeare—but he's never heard of William Hazlitt. At least, I think he said "No." He may have said "now" or "know."

I hope Claude interprets my requests to repeat himself as proof of my politeness. But the London Cab Lecture Series isn't about manners; it's about firm views on what's wrong in the world today. Downward trends in quality of life engineered by politicians who have ignored their electorate and global threats to them. Claude's speech is far from subtle either phonically or socially. It's anti-immigrant, anti-Arab but he's just as pissed off at America. Bush should have left them alone, now they're after us instead of each other, Claude reasons. His forcefulness gives the impression the least I can do is personally convey his views to the president since Claude can't leave his cab. I'm obviously at loose ends if I can spend time visiting museums.

Created in 2000, the Tate Modern revitalized a disused power plant rendering its signature smoke stack a harmless anachronism. Where once coal-fueled turbines were dark and satanic, natural light floods the Turbine Hall. A ramp descends below grade to the gallery's front door. Now the vast space inside the multi-story brick structure has acquired artistic power.

As an art student, I couldn't have afforded cab fare anywhere. "The last time I was here was in 1975," I tell Claude. From the tower of St. Clement Danes through the fresh air of the Victoria Embankment, a peal of "Oranges and Lemons" follows us.

"I thought I recognized you," says Claude. Funny guy. Impossible accent. I had an easier time with Mr. Khan and he was from Pakistan. We're almost in Soho, about to pass the luxurious Savoy Hotel.

Monet might have shed a tear for the Tate Modern. Not because of a favourite work hanging there but for the recent disappearance of the only good reason he had to leave his beautiful gardens in Giverny to paint the view of Waterloo Bridge and Charing Cross Bridge from the fifth floor of the Savoy Hotel: London's uniquely filthy air.

He did over seventy paintings of these smoggy scenes and about twenty of the Houses of Parliament. Monet's obsession was light. Ironically, the unhealthy particulates of airborne coke refracted light waves in extraordinarily beautiful ways. Monet's stated goal was to "paint the air" but I think his basic intent was to control nature and fix a moment in time of his own choosing.

Light's ephemeral presence led his brush from studies of haystacks to the riotous twilight sky of the Thames and finally to a two-acre body of water he created by diverting water from the Ru River to his home. (Monet's neighbours weren't happy about his retirement project: they believed his exotic crossings of flowers and water lilies would poison their own water supply.)

For forty years he developed elaborate pathways with bamboo, rhododendron, apple and cherry trees; the garden's heart was a footbridge inspired by a Japanese woodblock print. From it, he hovered over *Les Nymphéas* (the Water Lilies) for twenty years. At the peak of his talent, cataracts clouded his eyes. Monet let subject matter drift away like his beloved flowers. Ten years after his death, his massive canvasses of almost pure colour, *La Grande Decoration*, were erected in the *Orangerie* in Paris—a greenhouse built by Louis XIV so the Sun King could eat oranges whenever he wanted.

The strokes of pale orange and blue in *Les Nymphéas* seem to hesitate as if there are layers of eddies, hidden currents pushing and pulling at the surface. How deep the pond might be, its boundaries or source—these are details outside Monet's interest and the painting's vast frame. The certain brushwork that set Rouen Cathedral vibrating, and the Houses of Parliament ablaze, has disappeared as if some other artist applied the paint. *Les Nymphéas* is pure painting, barely representational. It's an experiment. At ninety, he's still searching. He seems to say it's okay to be indefinite. Nature is.

If Monet was enthralled by light, Pablo Picasso's bondage was to women. Not the fetish, necessarily, but to sex. Women held his imagination captive for his entire life. In 1901, when Monet was living in London painting scenes of the Thames and befriending other Impressionists like Whistler, Picasso arrived in Paris. The twenty-year-old Spaniard couldn't speak a word of French but he knew Monet's language. He came to absorb and surpass every artistic vocabulary of the twentieth century. Until labels on soup cans became art.

What's shocking about Picasso's erotic etchings at the Tate is that they were done by an octogenarian. In one print, he draws himself standing barelegged in boots exposing a penis the size of a pneumatic drill, in a group of gentlemen in top hats and tails. They ogle rotund women who spread their legs as if opening a door to knowledge deeper than intercourse. In another part of the picture he is the observing artist, brush in hand, crouching before the whole scene for a better angle—except that his white head is a cloud that has drifted from his body. It's a fantastic comment on mortality. Picasso knows his procreative time has passed—the women wear their hair circa 1900—but he's not the least bit reluctant to describe what he misses most. Life's good. He seems to say that between birth and death it matters not with whom we couple, but that we keep coupling.

The thing that's stayed in my mind about Picasso is the fearless variation of his lines. No hesitation, this is an engraving. He must have had a picture in his head, one he's certain we can be made to see. In my case, it has taken a few years.

On the day Picasso turned ninety-one, our art history professor dimmed the lecture hall lights and placed a muffin with a lit candle beside the slide projector. We rolled our eyes as he led us in "Happy Birthday." Picasso was, in our view, a parody. Art was in paralysis or suspense. Painting was certainly dead. Sculptors were digging holes in the ground and wrapping buildings in silk. Even Andy Warhol's fifteen minutes of fame were far from certain.

Picasso's drinking buddy, Alberto Giacometti, hangs out on the Tate's fifth floor. Giacometti's copper-cast women are also on pedestals but that's about all they have in common with Picasso's muses. If Monet had lived long enough to see Giacometti's dark world, he would have believed Earth had left the solar system. We're lost in space. Human life is what you manage to scrape together out of thin soil. People are faceless creatures barely present. A Giacometti-built figure could not be more tentative. But one thing is certain: even in groups, living is a process of withdrawal. Giacometti's literary buddy, Samuel Beckett, asked the sculptor to design the tree prop for the 1961 Paris production of *Waiting for Godot*. A critic made the comment that there wasn't much to the stage setting. Giacometti replied, "Look at the shadow."

A chill went up my spine when I read that caption. One day not long after Erin died, I stopped the car in front of a dead maple at the end of our lane. It was spring; the tree could no longer hide. The living trees had sprouted green ornaments. I'd thought about cutting down that maple a hundred times but if I had its shadow would have disappeared.

How like museums are memories of Erin. I prefer Picasso but I understand Giacometti. The cab reaches Trafalgar Square. I wish the two Claudes well.

In the morning, I scurry through Soho under a sky swollen with rain clouds to my last stop, the British Museum. Hundreds of others share my idea to get there early. We roll across the courtyard over the marble floor of the renovated interior like wind-up toys.

In the main galleries stand fierce, bearded Assyrian demigods. It's corny, but I can't resist taking a picture of the dead kings with a sleepy security guard who folds and refolds his arms, his eyes fluttering as if he's had it up to here with Hellenic and Mesopotamian cultures. But his guests are no more worldly; roving bands of Italians, Chinese, Swedes, and Americans consider the Elgin Marbles and other exhibits like they were cruising end-of-aisle displays of specially-priced merchandise at their local supermarket.

I wander to the upper gallery where an exhibit has been curated on behalf of Wellcome Trust.

Banners hanging from the highest point of the interior arcade advertise the sponsor's subject: "Living and Dying." The handout explains why we might be interested: "People around the world seek well-being for themselves and for their communities in many different ways." I can still bail, but I walk up the stairs into the show, trance-like. Instead of the exhibits, I will study my fellow visitors, I decide. This strategy works well until I glance at a photo of the Nicobar islanders' burning barges. There's a real body in that pyre somewhere. They didn't hold the funeral as a cultural photo op. Suddenly, stimulated neurons fire up my own pictures of burning—the candles at Erin's funeral. Try as I might, I can't emulate the appropriate educational detachment of a young father and his seven-year-old daughter whose noses are pressed against the glass. More than anything right now I'd like to feel mild fascination for Mexican Day of the Dead figurines, and affect a casual "isn't-this-interesting" reaction but I find these exhibits horrifying. I am mowed down by invisible machine-gun fire. My eyelids bat like windshield wipers. Before people around me wonder if I'm related to these grieving villagers, I steal out the room, down the stairs, headed for the merciful relief of the previously shunned souvenir shop. But before I get there, I cast my eyes at the floor where I read a sort of slogan or mission statement for the renovated part of the British museum: "And let thy feet millenniums hence be set in the midst of knowledge." That it's set into a stone floor—not in a traditional overhead frieze—is a clever idea, made more so by the chosen words. People walk over them all day probably never knowing that the line is from an 1834 poem on suicide.

Lord Tennyson's best friend and his sister's fiancé, died suddenly. The poem, entitled "The Two Voices; or, Thoughts of a Suicide," starts like this: "A still small voice spake unto me, 'Thou art so full of misery, Were it not better not to be?'" one hundred fifty-four stanzas later Tennyson doesn't really settle the debate between the pro and con voices. He went on living, of course, and became immensely popular in a time when people actually read poetry to each other and grieved for best friends.

I'd ducked into this London museum to escape grief and yet everything I've seen seems related to death. Why can't the Heavy Thing leave me alone? I would have preferred to remain just another visitor who thought it was a charming quote about knowledge but I had to have a coffee in an Internet café and dig it up.

In Chinatown it is dark as night.

My afternoon agenda was to try and meet the man for whom my hotel is named but I skipped out on that plan. How instructive could William Hazlitt's life have been? On second thought, I think I'll let the man rest in peace. Somewhere along Shaftesbury Avenue, I give existentialism and art the slip and squeeze into a Chinese restaurant for a glass of Chablis and fish and chips. The skies have opened up and it's finally raining.

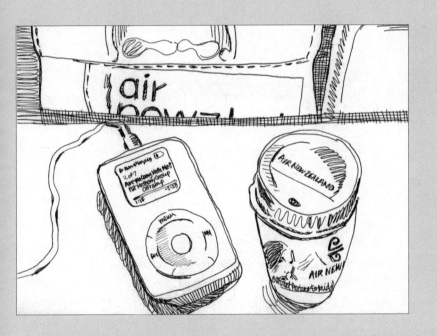

Sorry I'm Not Blonde and Forty

I have grown old in places where I never meant to stay.
—Terrence Mallick, *Sansho the Bailiff*

"YUM YUM YELLOW."

My seatmate is probably not a marine biologist, but Geraldine is certain sharks will be attracted by the colour of our life jackets if we try to land in the Timor Sea. That is an enormous, unmentionable "if." Seatmates do not want to think about the possibility of death, much less strike up a chat about it with a total stranger. But *we* do. We talk about the probability of death. But that was after quite a few drinks.

The whole idea—that the community of crew and passengers on Singapore Airlines Flight 123 would consider landing on water—is suspect. To begin with, the verb "land" doesn't fit the extraordinary circumstances being hinted at on my video monitor. If I was an engineer of airframes or a buoyancy expert, I certainly wouldn't want to think about centre of gravity, normal gross weight, air speed below 130 knots, the stability of water on impact, and so on. It's not a real possibility. I want that pre–takeoff drink, a little BBC *World News*, and some stimulation of concern for disputes and calamities I'll never hear about again. I follow the red line streaking across the screen over Eurasian territories and scrutinize our air speed and outside-temperature read-outs wondering what possible use this has for me. I want to settle back for a twelve-hour snooze from London to Singapore in the infinitely adjustable cocoon-like lap of luxury.

The alleged water landing demonstration ends. I am relieved to learn that contact will inflate the life jacket; I wasn't sure I'd be able to blow into the plastic hose after three meals and the flavourful Shiraz from the Yarra Valley. I make a mental note to eat less on airplanes for safety reasons.

"Sorry I'm not blonde and forty. My name is Geraldine. Call me Kerry," she says, watching a glass of Australian Champagne being placed before her like the opening gambit of an international chess tournament. I fail to react to the professional urge to explain only grapes from around Épernay can be called Champagne. It's an obtuse, possibly alienating response I am able to restrain in the nick of time. A month has passed and the ceaselessly fertile *terroir* of my marketing brain has been withering for want of moisture. I'm grateful for a full-fledged, entirely unpredictable conversation with anyone.

"Champers?" says the attendant who is beaming as if she'd just won an Oscar. Champers. Maybe that's what non-Champagne champagne producers should call their sparkling brews. Champers for me. And no more talk about death.

Please.

Somewhere around Tashkent, both of us satiated with fresh developments of the global condition and feeling like masters of the universe, Kerry tells me her life story. A childhood in Somerset, the War, best sleeping techniques on twenty-six-hour flights, her children's names, her children's children's names, best places to stay on the Gold Coast. She should know—she and her husband had a motel chain which they sold six months before Charlie died. "Never knew he was sick," Kerry tells me. She pauses and I know what's next. She'll ask if I'm married.

We'd been having a nice chat about the quality of Singapore Airlines and the quality of Australians ("Greatest people on Earth. And I should know—I'm English."). The marriage interrogative snaps me to alertness. Like: "On your mark, get set…" I know what happens next. Kerry will cry and I'll try to reassure her that I've got plans and my future is bright, trying hard to steer my story away from her swollen eyes.

I can't bring myself to tell Kerry the truth. She's already told me she's on her way home from her ninety-year-old mother's funeral and that her husband, whom she loved and with whom she had three kids, died seven years ago. This doesn't have to be *quid pro quo*.

"Cancer," I say.

"IF WE DO NOT EXPECT
the UNEXPECTED, WE
WILL NEVER FIND IT."

— HERACLITUS

Cutting Remarks

Despair is perfectly compatible with a good dinner, I promise you.
—William M. Thackeray

METAL KNIVES ARE FLYING into Bali, but not on return flights like this one to Singapore. I don't mean literally, under their own power, of course. They arrive with the meals. It's quite alright to use a knife when eating on a plane in Indonesia's airspace. But Singapore, like most countries in the world, has asked airlines to refrain from offering access to metal knives at mealtimes. Or at any other time. So I speculate there must be quite a business in used airline knives down there in Denpasar, Bali's main port of entry. Since they can't fly back with them, I imagine Singapore Airlines have quite a cache of silverware. The world's best airline got to be that way through deliberate and unselfconsciously luxurious service. Not surprisingly, the food's very good. There's a lot of starched linen involved, things placed correctly at ninety degrees. You can have seconds. You can have two desserts. In first class, you get a lovely rose in a porcelain vase. Singapore Airlines wouldn't just stow prohibited cutlery in galley compartments on flights back home. They'd deal with it. And profitably, too. I didn't see any during my stay, but the knives have definitely infiltrated Bali's local economy.

Meanwhile, what to do about the substandard plastic knives?

Fears that intemperate cuisine purists in the business- and first-class cabins might turn mutinous upon learning, as I did, that on this flight there would be no solid silver knife to deal with the guinea fowl pan-roasted with milk and marjoram or the salt-roasted chicken wrapped in pancetta, are plainly paranoid. But you never know. Since 9/11, you get plastic knives, which it turns out have pretty much the same tactile strength as their hefty predecessors. Plastic knives are a reasonable precaution. A little thing; it's not even a compromise. You move on.

Except if you work in food services at Singapore Airlines. Here, plastic knives are a significant reminder to chefs that they can't entirely control their product presentation, which, as far as I know after three long flights, is predicated on delectable food served continuously from takeoff to landing.

As it happens, Bali to Singapore is a two-hour meal and from the moment you sit down, trays levitate before you. With solicitous, graceful gestures and radiant smiles, attendants are consumed by an appetite to see you eat.

"It all looks so good," you say, declining the pre-appetizers. A shame, their eyes say. The airline chefs (two words that are not generally seen together) probably love the idea that while in Indonesia their customers can grip a finely honed piece of sharp metal and eat a civilized meal in complete luxury, instead of feeling that passengers can't be trusted with knives outside the home.

Singapore Airlines, I muse. For food lovers in a dangerous time.

Why Balinese authorities allow knives is beside the point—I don't want to involve myself with tricky geopolitics—but inadvertently they have raised a cutting-edge issue of "existential marketing." Not: Why are we here? (We are here to eat.) But: "Why isn't it here?" The knife issue might become a business case for worthwhile study by the executive MBA candidates surrounding me. The question is this: Do you go ahead and offer the real knife on the first segment of a return flight, and risk annoying your customers on their return with a fake knife? Or do you just live with the inconsistency? Life's unpredictable, but marketing's all about consistent portions, logos, and meeting expectations like a long-lost relative. In simple terms: is it okay to wing it?

Throughout Singapore "winging it" is discouraged. I read some place (probably in their in-flight magazine) that no one may spit or jaywalk on city streets. I didn't see anyone do it, either. I mean if a person suddenly started choking on some food in Singapore—I believe you are still permitted to eat out-of-doors while walking—the police force would likely turn a blind eye to a lifesaving spit.

Jaywalking, however, is a different story. What I saw along the treeless sidewalks of Orchard Street, where everyone shops in Singapore, were formidable (but jumpable) concrete barriers. Assuming a shopper wanted to purchase a luxury watch—had to have one more ruby-encrusted woman's Tissot right then and there—that person might hop, skip, and jump to the far side of the busy four-lane avenue. But it's hard to say what reaction Singapore drivers might have to such a crazed, culturally detached individual. Holiday Inn ads used to claim the best surprise is no surprise at all. That must have been written after a trip to Singapore.

Real and imaginary conflicts in the republic's social, political and commercial spheres have been usurped by a simple imperative that transcends all differences between Chinese, Malay, Indian, and European communities: we have to make a buck. Service industries like airlines and hotels transformed a small dot in Southeast Asia with minuscule natural resources into a global seaport. Singapore is a business hub to prosperity itself. And dullness. Dullness and cleanliness are the only civil circumstances Singaporeans have ever seen or thought about. The alternative is messy individualism, uncertainty, chaos. Like North America, say.

For Singaporeans, dealing with outsiders from the US and Canada can challenge their polite demeanor, as I experienced in the back of a cab. My driver, firmly fastened behind the wheel, got so frustrated with my dismissal of the seat belt lying limply beside me he launched into a tersely worded lecture on how my cavalier attitude was endangering his life. Government-sponsored billboards along the roadways confirmed (or inspired) his reproves. Announcing the upcoming Chinese New Year celebrations, they said (I've forgotten the exact headline), "Have a good time, but be self-vigilant because there's always a danger something criminal might happen as a result of your unrestrained pleasure-seeking." I harnessed my seat belt.

Back to Flight 143: technically, the Republic of Singapore, where I was disengaging from a sustained meditative focus, fiddling with the knife. It's not a good thing for a flight attendant to see a foreign passenger lift up a knife and study it for a little longer than is needed to establish its appropriate—or approved— use. And worse if Seat 12A smiles quizzically at her, which I was.

My mind was being diverted from the plane to the kitchen of my married life. On my airline plate was a message, a printed notice, the size of a fortune cookie message, apologizing for my plastic knife "owing to varying standards of local authorities" and urging me to enjoy my meal anyway. Something about the dullness of the knife's design, not its controversial edge reminded me of a spring day when Erin had come home with new cutlery. The forks, spoons and knives had playful, iron fiddleheads for handles. I burst out laughing. It was another one of those uninvited connections between my past and the present.

Sometimes you just have to laugh. That's real luxury.

66 WE ARE NOT HUMAN BEINGS HAVING A SPIRITUAL EXPERIENCE, WE ARE SPIRITUAL BEINGS HAVING A HUMAN EXPERIENCE. 99

— PIERRE TEILHARD de CHARDIN

INDONESIA 5000

The Last Picture Show

This external universe is a cinema show to the realized man. He lives and works in it knowing that its objects and bodies are illusionary appearances just as an ordinary man knows the scenes and characters on the cinema screen are illusions and do not exist in real life.

—Paul Brunton

What happened? Is the picture over?

—Bob Hope, *Road to Bali*

ESSENTIALLY THERE ARE TWO true things about Bali: tourism is dead and God is everywhere.

The first fact has only recently occurred. The second I had come to verify firsthand. I arrived in Denpasar, a sprawling dusty city as parched and paved as Los Angeles, during *Kali Yug*—the fourth and final Hindu epoch which marks the end of the world.

The Airbus was one-third occupied: an even mix of locals returning home for the weekend and mostly sallow-coloured expatriates wearing madras sport shirts and gigantic watches. The lone tanned businessman in the seat ahead of me chuckled at the on-board arrival announcement. "Whether you are here on business or tourism, welcome to Bali." It was "tourism" that prompted the laugh. The purser smiled helplessly, stopping short of a giggle, but he was tempted, I could see, in the way shared nervousness invites jokes at funerals.

You could hardly blame them. The announcement was pathetically out of date. It was obvious as we walked into Denpasar airport that something catastrophic had happened and that its presence haunted the corridors and empty spaces; the customs hall echoed like a condemned building waiting for the wreckers to arrive. But they'd already been. Even in death the "Smiling Bomber" (he grinned idiotically throughout his trial) had demolished Bali's economy. Above the blast site at the Kuta Beach disco where over two hundred people died on October 12, 2002, the senselessness of the tragedy settled like a mushroom cloud visible for miles marking this beautiful haven as a toxic place.

The official acknowledgement by the Indonesian government consisted of small billboards promoting tax incentives in neighbouring Java, by a strange twist of dharma, the home of the Smiling Bomber. There was no mention of Bali being back to normal or the traditional iconic photo of a minister of tourism wishing foreigners a happy holiday.

Left to my own devices, I interpreted the expectant faces of merchants, and their clamorous overtures for monkey-forest tours, or the best rate on rupiahs, as a bad misalignment with reality, the way the soundtrack of a movie can get out of sync with the picture. It was as if no one had told them the tourists aren't coming back. Or maybe they knew something the rest of us didn't. Be prepared for the gentle, constant happiness of the

Balinese, people told me. There are all kinds of happiness, but this was either spectacular optimism or a colossal delusion.

Bali is where Erin and I would have gone on our honeymoon, had I been able to persuade her that the cost wasn't that high but of course I couldn't—it was—and we didn't go. When we first dated, I couldn't get over how frugal she was. She had a sense of humour about it, though. Like the old black kitchen wall-phone she'd had her grandfather glue to her car dashboard. That was her cell phone; she made a big show of it at stoplights to the amusement of drivers beside her.

Despite his short arms and legs, which has to be frustrating for a professional driver, the man behind the wheel of my pre-arranged cab couldn't be more content. No power steering, no air conditioning; the Corolla is stifling and the dense heat is just getting started. Wayan speaks English haltingly but has enough courage to ask me if I am married and if I like Bali to which I've said, "Yes," twice. It will be two hours to the beach hotel in Yeh Gangga, not really on the tourist circuit—or what had been the tourist circuit—and my marital status is a subject too rich in implications for a casual chat. Sometimes grief is more companionable than people.

We slip out of Denpasar, passed frequently by the speedy *bemo* minivans, heading west along scooter-infested roads that are lined on both sides with shops, some barely more than a plank resting on a rickety frame, until we have chugged further than the last astonishing, random inventory of fruits and vegetables, car parts, shirts, DVDs, bolts of vivid cloth, jugs of homemade juices, and teak carvings of Indonesia's sacred and profane personalities. Everything is on sale but liquor. Once on the country roads, I hang my arm out the window, directing cooler air to my head. Then I settle back as the opening scenes of Bali fade up.

In the absence of subtitles I skim through a guidebook on Hinduism I picked up in Singapore. I learn that *Kali Yug* is the final revolution of the wheel of life. In mortal terms, a period of one million years, or one-thousand "divine" years. *Kali Yug* is the beginning of the end and the end of the beginning of humanity, the universe and anything else that might be in it. It's the ultimate reincarnation, epic beyond imagination, the crash of crashes followed by a forced reboot of the cosmic hard drive. Not only will *Kali Yug* eclipse existence some time soon but the world has had countless *Kali Yugs*. Over and over again, birth then death.

I doubt this is the last day of the "Age of Darkness," and that's a good start to any prolonged contemplation of existence that my new destination encourages, but there is no way to know for certain. Still, one million years means the wheel of life has a fair amount of play in it. And it isn't as if I have seen any tote boards counting down to the Apocalypse.

I surmise that Hindus on Bali (98 percent of the population) need no such disincentives. They are more or less engaged on a daily basis balancing cosmic concepts like dharma (our fate), and karma (actions and consequences that affect our ultimate spiritual progress) in the same way that I might watch the gas gauge and study the landscape to coordinate my next fill-up. They have a practical, all-purpose tool called *susila*. Think good thoughts; talk honestly; do good deeds. It comes with a lifetime guarantee: reincarnation.

Reading this, I reconsider my perception of the airport merchants. Maybe their behaviour makes sense. This new information (or ancient depending on your religious affiliation) couldn't be more explicit. Inexorable forces beyond our control shape existence. So, on the road of life, as on the road to Bali, it is much more than reasonable to accept each new condition in which we find ourselves; it is the only way to make spiritual headway. To analyze a particular event as happy or sad is pointless. It's like believing you have the ability to undo the event itself.

No matter how destructive and sad, suicide is an infinitesimal moment barely perceptible within the cycle of life. Not trivial due to individual circumstances being less significant than cosmic ones, but because the sum total of what we do as individuals over the course of our countless, successive lives on earth is far more important. Prosperity and poverty, ambiguity and certainty, bliss and despair, states of heart and mind are fleeting. Nothing lasts forever, except us. This helped me a few days later when I was again asked—this time by Edi, a hotel waiter—if I was married.

No one I encounter running, including the priest in Yeh Gangga, needs to elaborate on the telltale signs of *Kali Yug*: greed, addiction to sensuality, and obsession with the body. Personally, two decades of running is living testimony to my attachment to the last sin and anyone in the industrialized world will unabashedly acknowledge the proliferation of the other two and, no doubt, lots of nonspecific wickedness, too.

I run each morning at dawn, before the incandescent sun stokes the air too fiercely. Through the villages between the rice fields or on the beach below the hotel bluffs, I wonder what the guy jumping on his scooter to go off to work thinks I might be doing in his town. Do the fishermen hauling their outriggers into the Indian Ocean mutter, "Great. *Kali Yug*'s here; there goes a guy obsessed with his body."

But I am always greeted with a smile and an announcement-like "Hello." I am an acceptable presence in their midst, my running as welcome as the egrets trolling for food in their rice fields. If this is *Kali Yug*, the struggle between good and evil is no more pernicious than the rains in late afternoon and as imminent as the dormant volcano of holy Mount Gunang Agung.

Sometimes I know where I am, how far approximately in time from the hotel to the temple of the dead ancestors at the edge of town or to the fishermen's huts on the beach. Sometimes I stray. Sometimes I get lost. And when I do, I blame Ganesha. Normally the appearance of a four-armed, powder blue elephantine-headed statue would stand out on a roadside, but being so ubiquitous in Bali, Ganesha's presence takes on all the conspicuousness of a mailbox. I have come to expect the god of knowledge and the remover of obstacles at every bend in the road and his reputation for reliability is intact. My dharma was temporarily stranded a few times last week by an unfamiliar intersection but people who now recognize me emerged as my mobile landmarks to point the way back.

There is barely a spot in the countryside unadorned by worshipful thought. The stone shrines in the rice fields, the flower and fruit offerings on village stoops left for local deities and mouldy food strewn on sidewalks for evil spirits (and eventually mongrels) are frequently matched by an elegant and powerful greeting. I enjoy the gesture of clasped hands upraised and the words *"Om Swatiastu"* (May God bless you) and the proper response *"Om, santi, santi, santi, om"* (May peace be everywhere). It gives me a way to interact on a level other than menu queries. Literally, the translation falls short of "I recognize the divine in you" but that's its real meaning. There is nothing to make you feel connected to another person than to say you see his soul, tucked away in a corporal container and that you know its presence is a divine, return ticket.

Suicide is problematic in Bali. Balinese Hindus believe *salah pati* (a "misdeath") sets your spiritual clock back as much as seven lives. After suicide, you are reincarnated to the point where you left off, karma–wise. Then, assuming you deal with the issue that defeated you, it's on to hell for an indeterminate period of time. The definition of suicide excludes *sati*, the custom of widows hurling themselves on the husband's funeral pyre. *Salah pati* didn't stop the last royal family in Tabanan, about six miles from my hotel, from stabbing themselves to death one hundred feet away from invading Dutch troops in 1906. The soul of a suicide faces difficulty in going to heaven and requires a special ceremony by the Balinese family to correct the problem. According to tradition, the self can expect to be reborn eighty-four million times. By then, one hopes the quest is over and Enlightenment is achieved. What a long strange trip it's been.

I have gone to the monkey forest in Bukit Sari, got a ridiculous deal on the money exchange and bought some traditional *kain* fabric with it. I walked a trail through a working stone quarry on a muddy river gorge still hand-cut by entire families like prospectors and visited a "typical" farm with more "homemade" crafts than signs of cultivated crops. But mostly I have stayed put. I am happy to read and think, write postcards, and try to research the personalities of the resort's statues and sketch them with help from Edi, the houseman. From my bungalow, I watch the patient progress of rice farmers planting in their fields of gold.

At the dinner hour, I am reluctant to give up the beautiful privacy of my bungalow, which is set near one of the foot bridges that crosses a stream from the communal rice fields; over my shoulder are the central mountain ranges where all Balinese ancestors live and in front of me, the watery plain of the Indian

Ocean. Around the corner from the reception courtyard and swimming pool you must climb a long, high stone flight of stairs that leads to the dining pavilion, a dramatic open space circumscribed by mahogany rafters and beams, thatched with native grasses. This view might explain the ubiquitous Balinese smile.

Once, during the afternoon, I crossed paths with a Japanese guest on his way to the pool. He was wearing a thick terry housecoat over a Polo shirt and slacks, an ensemble reminiscent of 1950s Hollywood; a peculiar costume on a day that was over 85° Fahrenheit and humid. His curled lip conveyed the internationally recognized expression: he was pissed off. Maybe caused by the absence of water sports activities at Yeh Gangga such as you'd find in Malaysian resorts or even at Kuta Beach. Maybe he thought he'd meet fascinating foreigners in Bali like me, although that seems unlikely. I said "Hello" full-voiced, as the villagers greet me. My fellow guest examined me carefully as if I was just another stone shrine on the property and kept moving.

Last night over a cup of syrupy coffee, the front desk clerk, Dayu, who at twenty-three years of age is already the mother of three children, came up to the restaurant. It was empty except for me. Dayu is an attractive woman with large eyes whose shyness constrains a wonderful, enveloping smile. At dusk, the sky has the iridescent quality of a Salvador Dali painting. Bats fling themselves through the sky, legions of tree frogs vault over our feet lurching towards the sunset. Tomorrow, she tells me, I will be the only guest in the hotel; the couple from Tokyo checked out early.

Nearby, Edi, the waiter, lets out a laugh that loosens the knotted *selandong* on his head. I join in. Even Dayu laughs. I say, "Now I know what it feels like to be rich man. I have the whole resort to myself." Their laughter covers my embarrassment. As soon as the words leave my mouth, I realize how stupid I sound. As far as they are concerned I already qualify as supremely wealthy. I change the subject to tourism and we talk about the hard times. According to Dayu, it has been over a year since occupancy was "normal." They've never had two rooms booked at the same time. They need more people. She says, "Too bad your wife didn't come."

When I tell Dayu and Edi why Erin will never see Bali, their reactions don't fit any of the usual forms like, "You must hope for the best," or, "Time heals all wounds." In fact, there is no reaction. There is a pause, a recalibration. Edi asks if I would like to meet a Balinese woman. Not then and there. It is just an inquiry to gauge my interest in remarriage. The juxtaposition comes as a shock but is not unexpected. It makes no sense to this Balinese man and woman that I am unmarried. Edi and Dayu readily accept Erin's death, but sadder to them is my separateness.

The next day Edi insists I meet his entire family, including his great-uncle who is the village priest. I can't come up with any excuses or face another postcard-writing session, so I go.

Edi's uncle is up to his eyeballs in work, accepting alms from every household in the village, one offering at a time, all day long. It is Galungan, the holiest week in the Hindu calendar, the celebration of the defeat of evil by the forces of good.

"They should be coming at the appointed time," he complains, but he smiles anyway, a smile that is a shrug. Edi's cousin, who couldn't have been more than eighteen-years-old, is introduced to me. He hands me an orange like a present. By now I think the whole town must know my story. The cousin laughs, even Edi's great-grandmother, topless and supine on her outdoor bed, resembling a half-dressed lizard, cackles. They're not laughing at or with me. This is the soundtrack to their life.

I draw a deep breath and inhale the aroma of cloves. Bali has restored my sense of smell.

Next door, some kid is terrorizing a dog. Then it is silent. We continue to sit peeling and eating oranges and watching the rain fall as if it's an important ritual. Just when I form the thought this silence must mean I should be going, Edi's uncle speaks.

Time, he explains, is as illusionary as people and events in this life. In making time, Brahma the creator's purpose was to draw attention to the inevitable cycle of birth, death and re-birth so that we might accept the end of life a little easier. So that we may live better, and by this I take it he means within a family, a town, the divine.

After a while there is no more to be said. I get a ride back to the beach on the back of Edi's Suzuki as the sky in this world turns pink. It's strange to see the roofless structures of homes and temples and not know which is which. At twilight, looking back at the village from my cottage towards Gunung Kawi temple and the mountains (where I have no doubt Balinese ancestors live) I realize Bali is so culturally integrated the island is an elaborate movie theater where all of life's drama is both observed and partaken. They are the movie. And the movie never ends.

" A SHIP OUGHT NOT
TO BE HELD by ONE ANCHOR
NOR LIFE BY A
SINGLE HOPE. "
— EPICTETUS

Sea Change

Perhaps everything terrible is in its deepest being something helpless that wants help from us.

—Rainer Maria Rilke, *Letters to a Young Poet*

WHAT ARE YOU READING?

There are methods that will annul a one-hundred-thousand-ton tanker but none for memory. I know this because Erin continues to look over my shoulder; I am studying an article about ship-breaking in a business magazine. It says steel from dead ships is being converted into cheap rebar to reinforce the concrete foundations of Asia's new skyscrapers. The demand is great. A quarter of the world's cranes are in Shanghai. The lead photo shows a skyline that glistens in the sun.

Memories thrive in the belief that they might be needed in the future—why is not the issue, they just are—so I remain bolted to a version of Erin and me, even as I travel on.

In fact, memory willingly polishes the year we built the

house, the day she left, the hour she died, like silverware that is too good for everyday use.

The more Erin overlooks, the more her qualities reflect either a warm glow or blinding light. I wonder if I can remember how she really was, any more than Erin could recall her true personality after lifelong attempts to withstand depression's powerful subjugation.

The year we built the house was the last time she had been happy in several years. It was also the saddest and, although neither of us knew it, the beginning of her end.

On the day we made our offer to purchase fifteen acres of rolling farmland and woodlots, the sugar maples were being tapped by a tenant farmer. Mike had farmed it organically for twenty years. He showed her the pond where geese and a congenial mink made their homes as well as the deer trails on the north ridge where we could cross-country ski. There was a new, mysterious history all around us, a story for every tree—excluding a particularly twisted ironwood near the road. So Erin named the property "Crookedwood." Having your own vintage syrup struck Erin as richer than square footage or acreage.

"Think of it: we'll have our own syrup for pancakes," she said.

"And Bambi for dinner," I said. We were thrilled by our good fortune. We were getting on with our charmed life.

Outside, I focused on tree-planting: Japanese maples at twenty-foot intervals along the driveway; tough Himalayan birches by the small bridge over the entrance creek; fast-growing larch and native spruce trees to cover the naked slopes of a magnificent berm, to deflect wind and snow from the house. The bigger the project, the happier I got. Inside, Erin knew exactly what would go where; she couldn't wait for the spring move and neither could I.

After Labour Day, the house quickly started to take shape. Our fathers, necks draped with digital cameras, got involved with hammers, drills, and miles of speaker wire and cable. They showed up so many times that the tradesmen thought the men were construction supervisors. Why else would anyone take so many pictures? Meantime, we traded in the Volvo for a serious four-by-four and started shopping in earnest. On weekends Erin paced off a van-load of brand-new antiques. Catalogues replaced floor plans. By Thanksgiving, it was clear Erin had more than a knack for interior design: she possessed a true gift. And we were spending too much money. But since Erin was as happy as I had ever seen her, I didn't care. We pressed on.

In the township, people talked about the strange house with a mix of pride and apprehension. A decorating-magazine photographer showed up one day and pitched us on a before-and-after story. The architect was becoming a member of our family. The garage being two stories and connected by a courtyard to the house; the roof, clad in galvanized steel and pitched in a high, dramatic way; the numerous windows and sliding doors; the semi-groomed landscaping—all indicated our plan was not to create a monster home or instant *faux* heritage but something special.

Derrick, the contractor, was frequently frustrated.

"This is a custom home," the architect reminded him.

"No, Peter. This is a *custom* custom home."

More than one person said it looked like Steve Martin's house in *Father of the Bride*. A Portuguese truck driver delivering lumber one frosty morning asked me if we were building a church. In a way, we were.

The week before Halloween, her father unexpectedly died.

Her sisters and mother were devastated but Erin was inconsolable. For months, her sadness equated the end of the world. By early spring, a year after acquiring the land, we were ready to move in and she seemed to be coping better. As it happened, it was my forty-fourth birthday and Erin forgot. Just one of those things.

Our marriage was beginning to reshape itself to fit Erin's moody disposition. What I was up to professionally—and emotionally—was even less important to me than it was to Erin. I craved a break from work but I saw it as another requirement of my unique, evolving partnership with Erin. She was sick, I was healthy. I fell asleep juggling cash flow, but I fully expected that she would "bounce back." But the normalcy we'd had before her dad died was long gone. Still, we made friends and took holidays; we had plans for the future. One idea was for a store, a sort of "Soho in the country," something like the house itself.

In time, her mood improved enough that she regained her domestic interests. She opened the store, which was a hit, but it cost a fortune to maintain.

I would come home at night in the summer to find her watering the gardens almost guiltily. We loaded up weekends with chores and entertained famously. I took up running trails in a big way. I worked hard to keep up with expenses and Erin's secretive ways of incurring them. In truth, I seldom said anything. We continued to have a social life, she with her city girlfriends and me with my trail-running buddies, but no sex life. We turned into brother and sister or a pair of supportive friends but the more we settled into our new place, the more we accepted the absence of passion or spontaneity. The memory of our first years faded like they never were. I worked hard and worried about Erin's health. I stopped noticing her indifference to me.

Six years passed like that. I never noticed.

That last night, after a month of manic episodes that destroyed the credit cards and ended with her attacking our retirement savings account, the night Erin called from the store apartment to say she wasn't coming home, I remember exactly what I said.

"Not coming home tonight or not coming home?" The second part of my question was deliberately provocative. She wasn't coming home. I remember the self-righteous indignation, that she was abandoning the long-suffering home team and I wanted her to know there was a line. And if you cross that line, who knew what might happen?

But really, the line—if there'd ever been one—had been crossed many times. Recklessness wouldn't result if Erin stayed away—it had been our daily diet. It was being brought to a grinding halt—at least for me. It was perverse: Erin saying, "Don't come in"; me lobbying for a continuance of an excruciating life we'd suffered for years. The ship of state was heading directly into the rocks and there was no one in charge. Erin was abandoning ship. At that moment I wanted a different crisis: adultery, drug addiction—anyone else's catastrophe. Nothing would have altered the doomed course.

Poor men break up tankers into bite-size steel pieces with hammers and saws and their bare hands. It is wretched, environmentally dangerous work. Ships are heavy with steel too valuable to be abandoned. In a First World port, they will rust, dispersing oil, insulation, and all kinds of toxic waste. It is too expensive to dismantle them in the US or the UK so they must come to Bangladesh and India. Ship-breaking is big business.

Where are we going?

Far below this flight where the Arabian Sea meets the northwest coast of India there is an obsolete ship that has almost reached Alang. Despite Greenpeace's best efforts to stop ship-breaking, the cruise ship, or freighter or oil tanker, will approach the beach this morning just as we land in Melbourne, looking for the tall red flags demarking the vessel's beach plot. The knowledgeable local pilot will guide the captain so he can run his ship aground at full speed. The tide will retreat and then crews of poor men will come to unthread every bolt, pry apart every joint, beam and wall, split the seams, and crack the hull and decks until the vessel is no longer a vessel but a mass of steel sheets and chunks.

You are tied to the idea of a home and marriage that never existed.

Then the steel will be slung on top of pickups or piled into dump trucks. Twenty-four hours a day, the loads will be conveyed to a blast furnace where ships are cremated.

66 LIFE IS A LONG PREPARATION
for SOMETHING THAT
NEVER HAPPENS. 99
— WILLIAM BUTLER YEATS

A Certain Distance

I wouldn't travel this far if there wasn't that spot, this place in my
heart, that vacancy waiting to fill up with belief.

—Rick Bass, *The Lost Grizzlies*

"HOW YOU GOIN'?" he says flipping through the ticket and
passport.

I think he meant, how am I going to get to Flinders Lane.
That's a very specific question—even within the repertoire of an
immigration officer—and skillful in its preemptive power. I have
to stop and think. There might be a shuttle-bus service, but I usually take cabs from the airport, so I hedge my bet.

"Taxi, I think."

He looks up at me with a facial expression that says, "I've
never heard that before." He's smiling and I think he finds the
Bali security exit stamp amusing. Or maybe I've just won the
daily Bali flight full-body probe. He smiles again and *Midnight
Express* comes to mind, Brad Davis sweating his way through
Istanbul airport, flattened on the tarmac, klieg lights blazing but

the documents are back in my hands faster than he can say: "No worries." Which he says.

Now I get it. He just wants to know how I am.

I wish I knew. I'm glad I don't have to answer that to enter Australia. Or to keep going. Maybe I will never get a fix on the questions like why it happened or what I should be doing with my life—or even how to finish this quest—because life itself is a moving target. It's true, I am ducking work in a way many people couldn't but it's not the great escape.

This moment in Melbourne Airport, contained in a swarm of vacationing couples, is subject to thousands of recollections, some true, some skewed. Most of them are about Erin. They are arriving and tumbling into each other like the bags down the luggage shoot.

What is it like to be surrounded by our lost life?

You might as well ask a fish to describe being wet.

We were immersed in her depression. Managing to keep her head above water was the best we could hope for and she knew it.

Every spring, she would lose weight and nosedive. At night, I would sit beside the bathtub, listening to her recap her day, a description of unremitting disappointment and personal failures—and try not to "happy her up." I gleaned a lot of true but useless information from my growing library on depression. Our intimacy became politeness. As if Erin was an unexpected overnight guest stuck because of a winter storm. It wasn't my wife visiting, but an unhappy understudy, who would be staying with me until they plowed the roads and she could manage the drive. I ignored the very first conversation we'd ever had on the subject of depression. Over my famous lemon-and-thyme chicken dinner, she told me her father had suffered through "dark periods" and alcoholism and that her late grandmother had been in and out of hospitals with "melancholia." Erin confessed the burden of being unlovable that had weighed down her whole life, and I picked it up.

Don't worry about it anymore. I'll love you. You seem fine.

Too many endings.

I realize now she knew how deep the disease went. Our last conversation wasn't about me resisting reconciliation; she was letting go.

I overhear an American couple talk about the renovations they're going to tackle as soon as they get home and an Aussie man and his wife are telling another couple how much they love "real Indonesian" food. The intimacy makes the hairs on the back of my neck stand up. I break out in pangs of jealousy. How boring their conversations are. How lucky.

At the taxi stand I walk into a vigorous culture clash between a supervisor and an overzealous cabbie. The cabbie has reversed into the head of the line without permission. He is likely Eastern European, maybe Romanian, judging by the accented shouting. The supervisor is purple with exasperation, almost hysterical. First he pecks the air with his index finger to get the driver back into his cab presumably so he'll move it; then he pirouettes to the ostensible first car in line to cut off a passenger on her way to the reversed cab with a dismissive wave of both hands. The supervisor's unfortunate uniform: aqua blue blazer, white trousers with piping trim, and a pink shirt—not exactly the outfit a gay man should wear if he hopes to maintain public decorum.

But why be concerned? These guys have met before. It's a long-running hit. They're actors with roles and they know what happens next. Already this story has progressed past the rising action to a denouement; the supervisor points a few car lengths away to a particular spot down the lane. We observe the new position and reform ourselves like extras.

I'm first up. My cabbie, a Sikh, unfazed by the entire performance, lifts my suitcase off the trolley, a gesture than earns us a melodramatic "Thank you" from the supervisor. The argumentative cabbie ignores our instructive example, thrusting both fists through his window with the kind of indignation reserved for an anti-Ceausescu rally and speeds off. My neighbours laugh. My cabbie turns to me:

"How you goin'?"

North, South, and Blue Poles

Common Snipe *Gallinago gallinago*: One is both thrilled and puzzled when he hears it for the first time, for it seems like a disembodied sound, the sighing of some wandering spirit.
—Arthur Cleveland Bent (1927)

PERFORMANCES AT EZARD RESTAURANT start each evening at 7:30 PM but so far, I haven't drawn a crowd. I've been concentrating all week on the contents of an oversized egg-shaped plate like a reduction heat, stirring up reality to get to its essence. The waitress thought I might be a food critic.

"Is everything to your satisfaction, sir?" Oh, yes. My disguise is intact.

The pen is on stage, my mind is the audience and tonight's main course arrives. As my pen traces the contours of five-star food in Melbourne, I can grapple with memories and other ambiguities. In aboriginal spirit-quest terms, my mind's "gone walkabout." Maybe this ritual is true sustenance, soul food, as the Voice would call it. Meanwhile, the pen knows its lines and confidently scrutinizes everything in its path, captivated by the artistic (or cosmic) implications of asparagus salad with poached quail egg, Persian feta, and hazelnuts toasted in truffle oil.

Taste this. Draw this.

The pen, the Voice, thank God somebody's working on this quest, my own spiritual roadies.

Just keep drawing.

I'm not much of a tourist. I'm preoccupied, putting it mildly. In these close quarters, the pen distances me from the noisy table of paunchy Scottish IT salesmen nearby. There's a nervous-looking forty-year-old couple at the next table (on their first date?). They all glance at me trying to figure if the scruffy-bearded man drawing his twice-roasted duck with succulent figs and glass of Bass Phillip pinot noir (unusual chocolate finish) is a food critic or full-blown eccentric. ("Looks to me like he's doing platescapes, Bruce.") Never mind, the show must go on.

Sketchbooks are starting to challenge clothes for space in my suitcase. I'm addicted to the sensation of drawing; they prove my whereabouts. The "why-abouts" still elude me. In London, I left the mailing to Eduarda but in Bali, I found a post office in Obud and so the process of drawing itself has continued to shed its grace on me. Like Monet's light, and like Picasso's sex, it has crowded out all other interests. But the pen's not infallible; on Degraves Street this morning I ruined a promising café scene with too many lines. I should have applied the efficient-effort lesson of my Rastafarian tennis pro.

Drawing is a thrilling way to cheat time but it causes an aggravating side effect: what to do with the extra time? The pen has been appropriating the hours I'd like to share with someone, a table companion, like Valerie, the hair stylist this afternoon in Flinders Lane.

"How you goin'?" she asked me. This time I answered with "Fine."

I guess Valerie is about thirty, based on her description of leaving Vietnam as a five-year-old. Ethnically, she's Chinese. And she is stunning. So I asked her out despite learning she lives with her boyfriend from Singapore. "It's really going nowhere and we've been together for six years, y'know?"

I was doing fine, she was turning over my offer of dinner at Ezard's, the scissors were snipping, my travel impressions were impressing and then I made the fatal mistake of explaining again why I wasn't married. I didn't have to lie as I did with Kerry, being a widower was enough. Valerie's tears took me by surprise but I managed to get both of us safely to the cash register. Asking her out was a bigger surprise. Being turned down was kind of a detail.

I skip coffee and walk upstairs to the hotel lobby.

According to Knowledgeable Phil (the nickname of the front desk clerk), there's more to nightlife in Melbourne than eating; I should try gambling at Crown Casino. It's the tallest, bluest building in town.

"It's becoming our landmark. You shouldn't miss it." He offers a brochure with a slick Las Vegas-by-night-style panoramic of Melbourne's casino district.

But I will. Tomorrow, I have a full day of pointless comparisons planned between my platescapes and the best that the National Gallery Victoria has to put up.

In the harsh light of day, I walk under Melbourne's skyline. It looks out of whack as if buildings from Dallas had suddenly sprouted throughout Kansas City. As if a person who's always hoarded money now wants to spend it as fast as he can on things like hair plugs, red Corvettes. Ostentatious skyscrapers slouch over quiet Victorian buildings like partying teenagers in their vacationing parents' basement with the sub woofer pounding, just begging the neighbours to call the cops. Hosting the Olympics in 1956 failed to wake the world up to Melbourne's vanilla charms so the city is madly scrambling, over-seasoning and undercooking the ingredients resulting in dubious landmarks like the casino and, apparently, the world's tallest apartment building, called "Eureka." It's all about finding yourself in Melbourne. In fact, the streetcars carry the tourist board's new ad campaign theme: "That's Me!bourne."

On the bridge over the Yarra, Knowledgeable Phil says look for a "very yellow" sculpture on the south bank. *Voila*, there it is: *Vault* by Ron Robertson-Swann looking like a large deck of bent cards, which is appropriate given that it's been shuffled all over Melbourne.

In 1980, *Vault* was installed to much fanfare in front of city hall. Citizens complained about its cost and non-traditional design. People were more accustomed to Queen Victoria or the odd governor on horseback. A newspaper wit immediately dubbed it the "Yellow Peril." The sculpture was a marketing disaster. For the sake of civic peace and quiet, the city sequestered *Vault* out of sight in Batman Park. For twenty years, it sheltered homeless residents. When this unintended (but useful) purpose drew media attention, city council retrieved the sculpture and parked it outside the Australian Centre for Contemporary Art. The decision pleased people looking for a place to park, but incensed the museum. As the Melbourne *Herald Sun* reported:

> "It is disrespectful, appalling and distressing," said executive director Kay Campbell. "We are at our wits' end over this.

We have put leaflets on the offending cars, demanded bollards be installed and even considered having someone down there permanently to collect donations." Ms. Campbell said she was horrified when she first realized motorists had found a new use for the sculpture. "It started with just one but word of mouth seemed to take over and it is amazing how ordered a system they have managed to institute," she said. But sculptor Ron Robertson-Swann was philosophical. "It shows, I guess, that Australians are inventive and forever pragmatic," *Vault*'s creator said.

The only Jackson Pollock in Australia is a few hundred yards past the "Yellow Peril." I enter the National Gallery Victoria, walking under its three-story waterfall entrance.

The National Gallery Victoria displays *Blue Poles, No. 11, 1952* in a room of its own. When the NGV made the purchase in 1973, anti-art Melbournians were vocal about a government that spent $1.3 million on a drippy mass painted by "barefoot drunks."

Thirteen years later, the public apparently grew up. After closing time on August 2, 1986, the pro-art camp demonstrated their support for a very nice 1937 Picasso cubist work called *Weeping Woman* by walking out of the NGV with it.

The ransom note was addressed to the arts minister of Victoria State. It read, "We've stolen the Picasso as a protest against the niggardly funding of the fine arts in this hick state and against the clumsy, unimaginative stupidity of the distribution of that funding."

A second letter was more insulting than the first: "Dear, oh, dear, Race Mathews, you tiresome old bag of swamp gas." It included a spent wooden match. The note threatened the destruction of the work unless the minister increased arts funding by

10 percent and implemented art prizes each worth $5,000 for Victorian artists under the age of thirty. It concluded, "Good luck with your huffing and puffing, Minister, you pompous fathead," and was signed by the "Australian Cultural Terrorists."

In response, curators removed the chairs of museum security guards who, in turn, went on strike for a day, demanding that their chairs be returned. A few weeks later, *Blue Poles* turned up in a locker at the train station. As for the guards, they must have won their grievance; I saw four chairs in the Pollock gallery. Not only has security improved but also the value of *Weeping Woman* (currently $70 million) and the four chairs are now made of leather.

What is art anyway? Perhaps it's a universal interpretation of the human experience for those of us who are artistically inadequate or too busy living to ponder the meaning of life, love, despair, or God. Once art was part of popular culture, but hasn't it become Cirque de Soleil—all show and no meaning? Christie's auctioned Van Gogh's portrait of his psychiatrist, Dr. Gachet, for $82.5 million. What if the treatment had worked—all that money down the drain? But Van Gogh killed himself and never sold a canvas in his lifetime. I'm surprised mental health advocates haven't invoked a sort of "Son of Sam" legislation that would divert auction commissions on suicidal artists' work to research and treatment.

I stood with five or six others (plus the Australian version of the bored British Museum guard) and considered *Blue Poles* in the same way I pray: rummaging for the right words, navigating between humility and terror, feeling inadequate but grateful to be alive, deeply mystified and hoping those around me don't notice. Four years after he painted *Blue Poles,* Pollock went out in a blaze of glory. He hadn't been able to paint for two years. He suffered depression his entire life. He tried psychotherapy on and off but drank constantly. Cause of death: suicide by car. Sometimes—and I think Erin knew this—you can't get past yourself.

Back to Fed Square by noon. It's become prehistorically hot. Melbournians have nicknamed the Ian Potter Museum of Art the "Fred Flintstone Building." There's a giant video screen carved into its asymmetrical slab wall. I'm watching people on their lunch hour watching Tyrannosaurus-sized Andre Agassi tear an eighteen-year-old Czech limb from limb; tennis fans are barely moved by the carnage of the Australian Open's early match-ups. Real blood and guts will come later in the week during semi-finals.

Meantime, here on the banks of the Yarra, all you'd have to do is add a few umbrellas, hooped skirts and top hats and this bucolic scene could be Georges Seurat's Australian picnic masterpiece. Over, on and beside the city's watery main drag, armies of runners and fleets of rowers are on maneuvers from dawn to dusk. The indolent few—lovers and retired people—organize lengthy meals under leafy canopies in Alexandra Gardens and Olympic Park. And if art, sports, family values, or romance disappoint there's always the Crown Casino, shimmering in the distance like an oasis.

But gambling is too close to home to hold any appeal. I bought a seven-day tram pass and walked everywhere. I want to visit vineyards and see the Great Ocean Way but I can't seem to organize myself. I must be leaving room for chance to initiate an itinerary in Melbourne. This, I'm sure, is the tell-tale sign that I've joined my pen on the walkabout.

"I think you're just bored," Brian says. "You must be to call me." I can hear my brother tapping on his keyboard and his kids squealing with glee. They're watching Monster Garage. "It's snowing. It's below zero. Do you remember how shitty that is? Go back to your trip."

So I have penetrated all three floors of Fred Flintstone. There was a gruesome exhibit by English-Australian painter Peter Booth, landscapes of faceless people in fiery, apocalyptic settings. "Have a nice day," the security guard said on the way out. I have watched more tennis on the screen in Fed Square in a week than in my entire life. I got the memorable haircut from Valerie and after, managed to sit through a matinee showing of *21 Grams*. I've mailed a batch of postcards to myself, even a few to clients. It was time for a road trip and to meet "Twelve Apostles."

The night before the road trip, I think: how is it that I set aside a connection with art for so long—even before Erin's illness? That I am drawing in Australia proves that Saint Lucia wasn't a fluke. And that maybe I can't kill my soul even though I ignored it for two decades. I draw, therefore I am. Drawing has been locating me more and more in the here and now. The cancelled stamps prove that moments count for something. They aren't all good necessarily. I wonder: do you only get your soul back when you admit to losing it?

The next day is bright and cold. I head out of Melbourne to the port area with Brent behind the wheel, a driver I've hired for the day. I've got the iPod adapter working finally. I'm feeling like those orange trees in Louis XIV's greenhouse deliberately starved for water by gardeners waiting for their monarch's command to bloom.

Following the west roads past enormous piles of woodchips loaded onto Japanese freighters, we play part of the Rolling Stones' *Exile on Main Street*. The Japanese, Brent tells me, need a lot of cardboard. Cardboard reminds me of boxes and boxes remind me of moving. But for the first time not knowing where I will be next year or next week doesn't generate a paralytic grip. I'm finally getting somewhere; south of Torquay we make the Great Ocean Way at mid-day. Wave after perfect wave, the breaks, like white tongues, lick the shore. The traffic is slow and it doesn't matter. Brent and I are talking about inconsequential things like wine and the last time he saw a rock show (Little Feat—Lowell George forgot the words to "Willin'") and turning fifty.

He tells me Australia's WWI veterans built the Great Ocean Way. I let that sink in. Was it a make-work scheme or salvation for these soldiers? Besides a great view of the south Atlantic there would have been little to encourage a highway from Melbourne, to say nothing of the cost to blast cliffs and span gorges and creeks. How many cars could there have been in 1920? But maybe it was more about faith. Faith that a highway would develop communities and growth, and maybe that by engaging in something bigger than themselves, veterans would suffer less.

Over monstrous bowls of clam chowder in Apollo Bay, I learn that Brent lost "confidence" three years ago. He wants to know if I did, too. Confidence wasn't my casualty, I tell him. Advertising is all about making it up on the spot; that I know how to do. What I'm trying to cope with is a wandering pen and the Voice, but I don't tell him that. I've told him my story and he tells me his.

He and his wife Cathy both worked for Ansett Airlines. When the airline collapsed at the peak of a national recession, they lost their jobs and pensions. They sold the house and moved to Gold Coast, a tourist town. Their two grown kids thought life for Mum and Dad was pretty good running a motel for a year, until a cyclone wiped it out. Brent's father died the next day. The family moved farther up the coast, near Cairns, where Brent and Cathy worked as Great Barrier Reef guides for wealthy Koreans. After a year the recession hit Asia, the tourists disappeared and then their jobs. So back to where they'd started married life in Melbourne in the parents-in-law's basement apartment.

Brent hit bottom because he thought he couldn't adapt to circumstances that kept threatening him and his family. But he was wrong. In desperation, he turned to drink: he gives guided wine tours of the Yarra Valley. His wife is a partner in the business. They've done okay. What they did was convert a hobby into a paying gig. I make a mental note that sometimes there are happy endings.

The cliffs above the highway to Apollo Bay disappear soon after lunch; the Great Ocean Way pulls Brent's minivan through the Otways (the national park where all the woodchips come from) and the rest of *Exile on Main Street*. Around Glenaire, the Otways reappear but now the land is a large meadow full of grassy hummocks. Finally, I see the Twelve Apostles, which was the whole point of our three-hour drive. It is impressive and wild. It has Grand Canyon drama to it and vicious sand flies. I follow the rhythm of the surf. It has all the time in the world to keep carving the shore cliffs and columns.

In the parking lot I notice a bird roosting on a lamp standard. It's not a gull.

"It's a snipe," says Brent. "They come from Japan."

What is it doing here? There was a male snipe on our property every spring. I looked forward to the weird whirling sound it made in flight. It was strangely loud but distant sounding, and always at twilight. In descent, it moved erratically, throwing off a pulse—*who, who, who, who, who*—an intense crescendo and diminuendo. The warmer weather brought me out to scan the treeline for his nightly arrival. It took time to spot the bird, being small and high. The snipe flew in Ferris-wheel circles; a courtship display. Look at me. I will make a good mate.

Brent steers us north on the Port Campbell Road through dairy country. I think: I won't find profound truth unless I follow that snipe. There and back, married or single, life and death, certain or faithless—it's all the same. I can't exempt myself from life's myriad circles anymore than a bird can. It still doesn't explain how Erin could but from this perspective, my life spent with her wasn't in vain—it's a point on a circle. The world will spin wherever I go, whether I pay attention or not.

This, then that. It's not all or nothing.

I say goodbye to Brent; we've arranged a time to see Yarra Valley wineries. That snipe is probably still perched on the lamp standard, his thin bill twitching like the second hand of a broken clock. Is he home or away? Japanese or Australian?

In two months, the snipe will take wing. He will find a place within the V-formation. After a six-thousand-mile flight, he will recognize the landmarks of a certain meadow in Hokkaido and know, without a doubt, he is home. He will perform the aerobatic ritual and instinct will tell him he is in the right place at the right time. Then he'll fly another six thousand miles back to the Twelve Apostles and instinct will tell him, as the Voice tells me:

You are in the right place at the right time.

The sun has already set in Flinders Lane. I am in my room, gathering my wallet and room key, getting ready for another dine 'n' draw in the hotel restaurant. Lately, I can really taste the food.

"TELLING THE TRUTH IS THE EASIEST APPROACH because THEN I DON'T HAVE TO REMEMBER ANYTHING."

— MARK TWAIN

Jewel Thief

If man did not suffer, the world itself might be destroyed.

—Giacomo Leopardi

I'VE NEVER BEEN SO FAR from home or so inside myself. Ten stories up, I had a narrow view of the Sydney Harbour Bridge (where for $245 people walk along its top twenty-four hours a day) and a broader one of my own trip. Travel is becoming my religion. I left a certain life and have seen and felt things that leave no outward trace anything has happened at all. Except for the drawings. It's been a long time coming, but the present has caught up with me as surely as the accidental spill of coffee this morning on my last fresh shirt before New Zealand.

If my soul is indestructible then Erin could not have destroyed hers, could she?

I earned this idea after sleepless nights and long days and it has ripened into a kind of reassurance. It makes no sense to say she is gone utterly anymore than I am dead in Saint Lucia, London, Singapore, Bali, and Melbourne but alive here.

I haven't talked to anyone apart from the concierge (who gave some truly bad restaurant recommendations) for three days. The big excitement this week has been the robbery in the hotel jewelry shop that took place during my run Sunday morning. Juho, my cabdriver, is the perfect guy to preserve my muteness record. I said, "Airport," and off we went.

Juho has the dispassionate face of a funeral director, saying nothing for several minutes until we enter a construction zone and the traffic funnels into a single lane. Then I get his life story. He can't put his finger on why he left Finland back in 1967, but Juho felt he had been living on the periphery of the world; he had ambition but life had changed. After WWII, things stalled economically. There were awkward questions about Russian sympathies in his family. His cousin decided to leave for Montreal. Juho came to Sydney. He remembers the Opera House being built. Juho must be about sixty-five, and judging by his barrel chest, once very strong. His meaty hands throttle the steering wheel as if it had a habit of challenging his supervision.

I remember a TV documentary on the Nordic passion—if that's not a contradiction—for Argentine tango, the dance of ill-fated love. I consider asking Juho if he, too, liked to dance, but I didn't like the connotation. I decide to stick with the international standards.

"Finland cold?"

"Finland cold."

I think I could have said, "Many baby-eating dingoes in Sydney at this time of year?" And Juho would have parroted that question, too.

Juho's cab slides over Sydney's potholes while his body oscillates side to side. The shocks are—well, there are probably no shocks. I notice this exaggerated motion because we are travelling slowly, at the speed limit, in fact. A black BMW 740i is inches from our bumper and the driver honks his horn, but Juho won't speed up even though there's no one ahead of us. Juho is removed from earthly concerns. Or he's quite deaf. My flight is hours away so I'm indifferent to our processional pace.

"How long have you been driving a cab?" I ask.

And this gets Juho stirred up: he never intended to be a taxi driver. It was supposed to have been a temporary thing. Was his destiny to be a ferry boat captain? Sheep shearer? Hunter Valley winemaker? Juho doesn't elaborate. Whatever he expected from Australia he is not going to say during my ride.

"I should have gone to Canada like my cousin," he tells me sourly as if immigrants there are less susceptible to taxi driving.

"Do you miss hockey?" I enquire. I am stretching the limits of my conversational abilities.

"No."

In a city jammed with attractions and natural beauty, I struggled to find something to do in Sydney. Instead, I stayed stranded on The Rocks. I watched CNN Asia so long I recognized the sequence of stories in the program loop. I ate and drew and most ironically, I tried to get away from tourists so I could see the city as it "really is." The truth is Sydney is really busy and I am a tourist.

The bike paths in Sydney's parks are patrolled by phalanxes of Pacific Islanders and Chinese tourists who approach individual runners as threats to their formations. Eventually, I ran up store-lined Macquarie Street then doubled back passing coffee shops, banks, and department stores (whose window displays try to incite travel to the Grand Canyon). I came back down to the steps of the Opera House, where, just for the hell of it, I reenacted the Philadelphia Museum of Art scene in *Rocky* when Sylvester Stallone leaps, arms raised.

At breakfast I read the *Herald* paying particular attention to all the local news, pondering what it would be like to live here. For a few mornings, I fiddled with bad sketches from the British Museum. I remembered the granite London sky, the limp flag, the chattering crowds. I wondered about the tall family of Scandinavians laden with books, the twenty-something couple who embraced and discussed where they would go for lunch, and the narcoleptic security guard. There were other details, moments I hadn't noticed, of course. Where are those people now and what are they doing? Will their memories be of a dreary day in January or the time they were in London when everything was going so well?

So this is how I know I'm coming back: I've commited to paper moments no one will ever relive. In Bali, a temple care-taker laughingly said my pen was my third eye. So be it. It's as unstoppable as Juho's decision to leave Finland, the schedule of ferries to Bondi Beach or the intention of four thieves who successfully made off with a $1 million worth of Rolexes.

I have stolen from myself but not from my soul. I am awake and I think Erin is okay. I have to get on with myself.

Abruptly, the road construction ends and one lane becomes three. The black car is able to pull alongside us then roar off but not before its driver, a mid-thirties male, expensive-looking tie and coloured hair, hurls a long curse ending with "pick a lane, you stupid old bastard." Reflexively, the cabbie adjusts his toupée but otherwise Juho is in his own world. He's not ceding an inch of the hard road to the airport.

" I WAS THE WORLD IN WHICH
I WALKED AND WHAT I SAW
    OR HEARD OR FELT
CAME NOT FROM MYSELF;
    AND THERE I FOUND MYSELF
MORE TRULY and MORE STRANGE. "
        —WALLACE STEVENS

The Forty-fifth Meridian

Thrusting a subject into the limelight is the surest way to destroy it.

—Henri Cartier-Bresson

THE HIGHLIGHT OF THE West Coast wasn't Punakaiki where I had a very good chicken sandwich on sourdough bread and watched more phantasmagoric surf, trekked up creek beds and decided after an unbroken period of happy *outward* observation (equivalent to three days on Earth) that this is what the afterlife must be like. Or California in 1900. I counted six houses in twenty miles north of the Pancake Rocks. Alan, the man who made the sandwich, was a friendly enough retired teacher from Auckland who told me he'd exhausted the local labour pool; that his biggest challenge was finding people who hadn't already worked in the café. A large dune blocks the view of the ragged coastline. You ponder the parking lot from the Wild Coast Café. There was something ironic about a retired man still working while the employable surf all day.

Hokitika did not qualify as a highlight, either—where I dodged three humid days attempting to draw the ubiquitous New Zealand silver ferns on a B&B farm run by Pauline, a retired psychiatric nurse and her Maori husband who'd retired from the department of conservation.

Hemi promised to tell me Maori stories after dinner but two other couples arrived the same night—an English software developer and his mathematician wife from Henley; and an ex-pat American from Manila, his Chinese wife, and their immaculately dressed two-year-old girl—so the dinner table discussion shifted to competitive rowing and daycare.

What stood out on the West Coast was a photo of a teenage boy on the kitchen wall. Hemi and Pauline pointed to the son who had died less than two years earlier but none of their other children or guests pursued the subject. I looked at Pauline and I surmised any elaboration was painful. The death of a child is not preferable to Erin's suicide. I can feel the silence behind their eyes. I see that death is everywhere and I feel sorry for their loss. I'm past wondering why me.

As a running route, Hemi said to try a loop a few miles down Stafford Road to a settler's graveyard. I did this, noting what a symbolic turnaround I'd been given, but after three attempts, I couldn't find the place. Maybe, I wondered one late afternoon bathed in sweat, death's tired of keeping up with me.

From Christchurch, my pen followed me down to Queenstown to better weather and will likely follow me, like Sancho Panza—Don Quixote's faithful sidekick—to the end. Through my mental fishing net, clogged with questions about Erin, my sidekick passes without complaint showing me how to execute landscapes, self-portraits, and platescapes. Maybe the postcards (which I'm now decorating with bits of poetry) are warnings to the old me, the one who waits faithfully at home.

Keep going.

In a Queenstown café by the boardwalk, I watched the crowds of camera-laden tourists for a while, then refocused my brain to watch my hand. There's no clue to a composition in its movement; the pen makes its own patterns like a planchette on an Ouija board. There's no telling when or why it may start or stop. Flipping through the sketchbooks is like watching the re-enactment of a Voodoo trance. But I'm residing, somewhere, in these pads of paper. Drawing is just something that happens, an unfolding equivalent to the random distribution of the day's events or the arrangement of stores in Queenstown. There's a kind of grace when I don't pick through the past or fantasize about the future. Both are pointless since it's all about now, the trip today or drawing this very stroke. It's a tough concept, the present tense. It's nearly impossible not to measure myself as retreating or advancing, grief–wise. And the unseen force behind drawing seems to say: there is no single path in life, no proper trajectory.

She's gone. Stop waiting for your life to come back like you used to wait for Erin's health. Keep looking.

In Queenstown, I have done day rides through local trails like Moke Lake Reserve and Arthurs Point, and cursed the heat, the elevation, the lack of trail blazes. I sat beside an Austrian grand-mother with skin tougher than my personality in a jet boat up the Dart River. I took a helicopter ride to Milford Sound with a honeymoon couple from Long Island and saw the drowned fields and thin curving of rivers running back to the Southern Alps and eventually to the sea.

If I could stop time, unravel the last ten years, carefully sepa-rating birthdays from arguments, overdrawn bank accounts from laughter, the real from the dreadful, pick through our inter-twined lives and examine every thread for telltale knots—would that show me a big picture like the jet boat or the helicopter? The lesson of my extravagant flights over water and land is: fill up this moment. A moment is all we ever get. Maybe for me the big picture is knowing I should try drawing it.

There is no dove, but no flood either.

The stars are relinquishing their night watch over the dusty, white shoulders of the Remarkables. Lake Wakatipu's surface resembles polished silver. A wisp of fog is playing hide-and-seek with the town's most famous resident, the steamer TSS *Earnslaw*.

It's a beautiful vessel, 165 feet long with a chalk-white hull and a blood-red funnel. My room literature says it's "a wonderful relic of the mining boom." The coal-fired steam boat has a cash bar, carries passengers for a ninety-minute cruise up the lake to Walter's Peak, five days a week. The cruise includes a light snack and if you want you can go horseback riding at a high mountain ranch or watch a demonstration of dogs trained as shepherds. In an hour from now, after everyone's had their breakfast, the cam-corders will be on patrol, probing and recording the town's quintessence. I should get a picture of me in Queenstown but at 6 AM, there's no one around to take it. A little while later, Sydney Street will fill with customers for extreme sports like bungee jumping, river sledging, rock climbing, cave rafting, rap (cliff) jumping, and "zorbing" (participants are strapped into an inflatable transparent plastic and rolled down a hill).

My last run will cover all of Queenstown except the ridge that encircles the town on three sides. For that I would need more time to deal with the fifteen-hundred-foot rise. At this moment, the gondola to Bob's Peak is nesting somewhere in the shadows. They say the view from the top is spectacular.

My footfall is the only sound in Queenstown. It follows me through the streets bulging with Internet- and smoothie-dispensing cafés and wine shops. I hook up with the gravel trail that snakes all the way to Frankton airport and turn around where the condos are thickest. I run past the skating arena on a rough track that too soon becomes a concrete path past the sailboats until I'm ready to sprint to the gate. Maybe it's just the endorphins, but I'm feeling more alive than I have in months. I am grateful to be here.

I think this as if the view of Queenstown was the feeling itself, an ephemeral idea likely to vanish if I loosen my grip on it. I saunter along Marine Parade to cool down. I hear the snap of the stern flag on the steamer. I stretch against the park's brick wall, and as I do, my mind as empty as it ever gets, refills itself with second thoughts: Why not stay here? Why ever go home?

Because you have to go on.

The street is stirring. Nancy, the housekeeper, walks by without recognizing me. The other morning I lingered so long at breakfast I strayed into conversation with her. She wanted to know how I could afford to come all this way.

"You're too young to be retired. Are you a drug dealer or a software developer?"

Right now I wish I'd paid more attention to money, wanted it more or just kept more of it. I've never been destitute, but now, I am essentially broke. I have no debts, but my savings are gone. I will have to work my ass off when, or if, I get home.

At the sound of a distant bus complaining up the hill, my concentration breaks. I turn in that direction and see a sign I hadn't noticed above the park gate: "1914–1918. Service above Self."

Two lines of raised letters set on a simple plaque in brick.

It isn't a gate to a park but a memorial to a contribution no one is alive to remember. A niche at the top of the arch contains a sculptural white vase with gold lettering. Beside a pair of small lyre-shaped buttresses and two red diamonds set in the posts, are the names of dead soldiers listed A to K and L to Z, but a "No Parking" sign makes them impossible to read from where I stand.

This street becomes Route 6, going directly to the booming tourist sites and the "red gold" vineyards in Gibbston and Cromwell. Before its construction in 1963, sheepherders, then later, gold miners and farmers along a hundred-mile stretch of the lake depended on the *Earnslaw* to get around. Launched in 1912, it was their only link to each other and the outside world. With a cargo capacity of about fifteen hundred sheep, the *Earnslaw* carried everything vital to life. Two years later, the steamer carried recruits from Otago farms and settlements as far as Glenorchy. The *Earnslaw* was the first stage of their journey from South Island to Auckland, and finally to the Great War in Europe. Of the eight hundred men from the battalion raised here in Central Otago, four hundred perished in a single assault at Gallipoli in August 1918.

I'm half-way home, half-way between the equator and the South Pole and still I wonder: where am I going? I imagine those soldiers wondered, too. With the first distinction from the dark comes dawn. It is light coming, not yet fully present.

Liquid State

ON MY LAST DAY IN Queenstown, I have picked up my first rental car of the trip; it's purple with the license number 666. I hope this isn't some kind of sign. I'm going to call it "The Beast."

It's not saying much but the highlight of humankind's presence in South Island, which I observed for a brief moment this morning, is the "Bra Fence." It's an inexplicable quarter-mile wire wall of lingerie. A few cars did pass me but between Queenstown and Lake Wanaka there hasn't been anyone to ask what it might mean.

I am riding The Beast far away from Queenstown's indefatigable tour busing Digital Asians, caravanning Superannuated Retired Teachers and the largest, youngest tribe of all, the Extreme Bungees. The Beast is a vestibule between me and reality, which means I have a spectacular view of the world at its best. It feels good to be moving again. There is something about driving alone in a car on a road you've never been down before that encourages thinking.

South Island is transcendently beautiful. At breakfast, the well-coiffed coffee wholesaler from San Diego told me that during the drive from the West Coast to Queenstown, his wife lost patience with him pulling over every other minute to photograph this misty picture postcard valley or that babbling brook surging with pure spring water.

To think the opportunity for beauty must be jumped on with a camera, because the experience will be assaulted any minute by the shock-and-awe force of ugly urban geography, is something I understand; indeed, it's the impulse coaxing me out of the car. At the approach to the next one-lane bridge, I want to stop and take a nice picture of this thick, green, wet world. In the foreground I'll frame-in one of those yellow signs with the name of the creek: "Joe," "Roaring Swine," "Random."

The only reason I am not setting up a tripod right now is because it's raining prodigiously, maybe biblically. This kind of rain makes a sunny day impossible to imagine. The Beast's flaying wipers do not make the narrow road any easier to see, but there hasn't been a car in either direction since Wanaka. When it started raining in the Cardrona Valley, the sun poked in and out over gold and emerald valleys that soaked up the drizzle until they sparkled; the hills were skewered with ski tows like a charm bracelet of crucifixes. At Hawea, there was a traffic jam in the sky. More clouds, bulging with moisture, followed me until I turned west at the Route 6 junction for the descent to Haast, then drifted east to be released somewhere else.

The rain always reminds me.

At the bottom of the manic-depressive cycle, Erin could not help but interpret everything, including rain, as portentous news. She reacted to an outstanding day of sales as if it were the expected, not impressive, result of hard work. A bad day of sales was the calm before the storm, a sign the store would ultimately fail, and that it should be closed before it did any more damage to us. She linked the natural deaths of our fathers, events sepa-rated by several years, as proof that bad things—rather than her mood disorder—perpetuated the depression. The world itself, she reasoned, made escape from depression impossible.

Our wedding reception took place on an overcast day on our back deck. Guests walked up the short distance from the church at the bottom of the street. When it came time for toasts, I made one to Erin's dad. I said I would always take care of her, not knowing, of course, what that might mean one day. I am a great one for sentimental gestures like toasts, but I meant it. The words were barely out of my mouth when a very loud rumble responded. Everyone laughed. But it never rained.

Papa Wemba is singing in my ears on the iPod right now. It is deeply sad music; the sort of ballad with so many tragic music cues I edited it from our CD collection so Erin wouldn't inadver-tently experience it. I remember reading somewhere that Papa Wemba was the son of a *pleureuse*, a professional mourner who cries and sings at funerals. What an odd profession; to think you could be trained to grieve while Erin's brain performed the same function automatically. The difference is that when Erin cried she mourned for herself.

The Beast crosses the one-lane bridges over the spitting creeks that feed the Haast River.

"Friends."

"Chink."

"Wrong."

In addition to the creeks, water gushes like little Niagaras from deep gashes in the Haast River gorge. It spurts in vigorous arcs that would dazzle firemen. At the sight of this aquatic dis-play, designers of fountains in public parks would weep in shame. Water sluicing down the sides of the gorge cannot dislodge mile after mile of silver ferns, mossy bricks in a perambulating wall of jungle. The highway gutters churn like hydroelectric turbines. On the high sides of hairpin turns are small sandbanks, the remains of constant backwash. To remind myself I am not in a boat, I glance into the rear-view mirror only to be astonished by the wake The Beast leaves on the viscous road.

The river and the highway coil and uncoil, the highway adhering to each turn of the gorge, the river flowing where it wants, due west. For an hour I've been observing the elephant-hide surface of the river. It lifts like white goosebumps, as the pounding precipitation enters the river subcutaneously like a trillion injections. At Haast, a small settlement on the coast, all that water will surrender itself to the Tasman Sea and I will stay with the highway that turns away from the south and head for Hokitika.

This week's schedule is loose: travel up the west coast of South Island and drop in on one or two world-famous glaciers. Not that frozen, compacted water has ever interested me; I'm going to see Fox and Franz Joseph glaciers because they're there—to paraphrase George Mallory. He might be appalled to know that today the glaciers are about as inaccessible as a Wendy's drive-through, weather permitting. I'll park the car practically beside the ice fields. Mallory's "Because it's there" quote was given to a reporter after an exasperating interview during which the famous English mountaineer could not articulate his profound need to climb Mount Everest. A few years later he disappeared in the attempt.

Before Edmund Hillary got to the highest point on Earth, he practised on Franz Joseph Glacier. Mallory may have been the very first man to ascend Everest, but Hillary was the first to get there and back alive. George Mallory would dismiss my adventure of unplanned circumstances as probably selfish and certainly inconsequential in the context of what can be achieved in this world. But, not to put too fine a point on it, Mallory is dead. Maybe he should have practiced on Fox Glacier. For me, there's still a chance.

The creeks keep coming.

"Grave."

"Epitaph."

"Paradise."

Still no cars. The highway is more like a conveniently cleared trail through a rain forest, which it is. It's easy to imagine the west coast as it was one thousand years ago when the Maori arrived.

Abruptly, the rain forest cedes itself to flat, sodden land. A "Welcome to Haast" sign appears followed by a dairy farm with animals stranded on small islands of dry pasture. Where glaciers co-exist with rainforests, New Zealand farmers have wisely introduced seemingly amphibious cows.

I pull into the parking lot of the tourist kiosk on the beach. It's closed for the day at 2 PM. Where exactly the leaden sky meets the Tasman Sea is obscure, as mysteriously unseen as Haast residents. If there is a town, it must be underwater. For all its signs permitting kayaking and surfing this is a dreary place for a beach party. To put it succinctly, The Beach Boys could not have come from Haast.

In The Beast I quickly finish my chicken sandwich, shaking the last of the coffee from my thermos. No matter what happens next, I've traversed the agonizing part of my post–Erin territory long enough. I'm going to enjoy the ride once in a while. Like now. The episode with Kelly in Queenstown has started me thinking in a new direction.

In Queenstown, I found Lily.

For a week I had been having dinner in the hotel bar. Eichardt's is a popular place with locals, especially the friends of its twenty-something bartenders: Jake, a quiet, agreeable Rugby player; and Kelly, an innocent-looking blonde who reminded me of every woman I'd ever been attracted to. To be surrounded by noisy, laughing, charming people without any obligation to talk to them turned the bar into a sanctuary. As I sat at the bar fixing sketches of a tour to Mt. Difficulty Winery, I watched life, like some visitor from outer space, detached but fascinated. Eventually my aloofness washed away in waves of cackling, good-humoured gossip mongering. It happened during a Kelly night.

Her friends Dee Dee, who worked at a local outfitters; Pam, a dark-haired beauty hidden under a wool cap; and William, a Colin Farrell look-alike were charging up the atmosphere. William was updating us on the latest escapades of the town's notorious newspaper reporter. I'd seen the guy in question and I didn't think he looked too much like a Lothario but what did I know on the subject of sex. He was balding and middle-aged. He wore a cardigan. I had been reduced to squelching lustful thoughts of Kelly and her friends. In fact, one night, Kelly had said I reminded her of her dad—never a good comparison. William spied my sketchbook.

"You're a bit of a scribbler yourself, Richard." He looked at the sketchbook and I handed it over.

Polite inquiries followed the sketchbook as it circulated the bar: where had I been, did I like New Zealand, that kind of thing. In turn, my pub mates announced their dream destinations. "Paris," said Pam and Dee Dee in unison. William thought gambling in Las Vegas would be pretty cool and Kelly chose the Grand Canyon. The conversation turned to opinions about local pinot noir; which central Otago winemaker was putting out the best—Akarua or Felton Road? Fierce defenses were being mounted when above the din Kelly asked for my pen. It was a strangely intimate thing to do but I surrendered it anyway. I could see Kelly intended to add something to my sketchbook.

"What should go on Richard's list of must do's?" she asked the bar. A wine tour of the Gibbston Valley. Jet boating on the Dart River. Paragliding over Queenstown. Please see Milford Sound. Absolutely do not miss Routeburn Canyon.

I listened intently, grateful for their suggestions, some of which I'd done, but as it was my last night I didn't want to spoil the mood. It was getting late. The other patrons had gone long ago. We exchanged e-mail addresses on scraps of napkins knowing we would never re-connect. Dee Dee, Pam, and William slipped out the front door, arm in arm. I looked over at Kelly who was still at it with my pen.

"You seem to be searching," Kelly said bluntly and looked up. She looked a little older somehow.

She hadn't recorded a list at all. Then I realized she'd drawn something. I made a vague, evasive comment like, "I suppose I am searching." I remembered the effect of telling the truth on the tearful hairdresser in Melbourne and the lie I told to Geraldine on the plane. But Kelly seemed not to care how I was reacting—or not reacting. She handed back the sketchbook. I saw a rough sketch of a calla lily; more Grandma Moses than Georgia O'Keeffe. It looked plump and well-nourished. The leaf ends curled elaborately like a costume in a baroque painting. A small stamen stood alone inside a heart–shaped flower bud. She wrote, "My Lily by Kelly. Qtown NZ. XXX"

"You've got to find your Lily, Richard."

"What does that mean? Is that a Kiwi expression?"

"No. It's a Kelly expression."

I'd drawn a blank. Maybe it was the Akarua or my age. What the hell: I asked her to explain.

"When I was a little girl I called all my cats and my pet Lab Lily. I named all my dollies, even Barbie, Lily. It was silly, I guess, but anything that I loved or that made me happy I just called Lily."

There was a long pause, and then Kelly mumbled that her drawing wasn't very good and I assured her it's all relative. Finally, she asked me a question but I had no answer to give. I put the pen back in my jeans and said goodnight.

She knows the answer.

In the car, pulling out of the Haast municipal beach, the meaning of last night's question hits me. My "Lily" is drawing. It always has been. I just found it again—after misplacing it for twenty-five years. There will be no death-defying bungee jumps to put an end to grief. The grief will go on, but so will I. Kelly, the bartender guru, has shown me how. And something more. I see the drawings for what I couldn't see, even decades before. They draw on my soul.

In Fox Glacier it rained solidly for four days. Up the road at Franz Joseph, it was the same story. The constant rain knocked out the cable service, all but the Weather Network and the Japanese info channel. I waited for a break, like a lot of people in the motel, so I could walk on the glacier but the spongy surface put an end to any hope of a tour. I suppose I could have waited a day or two longer for the weather to dry things up. But it was time to go.

On the day I left Fox Glacier, I drove to a restaurant near the beach because the owner of the motel said it offered an excellent view of the glacier. A glimpse was all I could hope for. The place was jammed with temporarily out-of-work tour guides. It remained overcast all day except for a brief moment when the clouds broke and there it was: Fox Glacier. It looked just like the postcard in the motel. Dramatically, a beam of sunlight trained itself on the ice field, which revealed the milky patina of a gigantic pearl. I had a thought suddenly that all the tears I'd shed over Erin had been collected and put on that glacier and that they could be safely left there.

Another creek. Another bridge. This one has no name. Maybe I've just crossed my own bridge.

Maybe I'm naive to believe I have had a Lily of my own all this time or that it can re-animate my life, but why not believe? Faith is the simplest component of belief, and I've been doing it for weeks. And weeks can become months. And months, I hope, years. Years of moments.

What's your Lily?

"THIS BEING HUMAN IS A GUEST HOUSE."
— Rumi

LAX Preparations

The real voyage of discovery consists not in seeking new landscapes but in having new eyes.

—Marcel Proust

ROMAN IS PUSHING HIS Ford Grand Marquis through the tail end of morning rush hour, along Lincoln Boulevard to a hotel on Pico across the street from Santa Monica High School. It's his fifth fare this morning but that's way down compared to normal.

"9/11," he tells me.

No one's travelling.

I am in no rush to get to the Four Points Hotel although I say to Roman it looks like the traffic is bad. The Auckland flight was early and a few of us managed to slalom through the Arrivals gauntlet, past boulder-sized luggage from Air Philippines and the incursion of Air China passengers. The US customs officer rotated the pages of my colourful passport and wondered aloud, in a voice burdened by the very idea, why so many countries? I shrugged, smiling like an idiot. This fits his entrance standards.

It is my last day of freedom. "Maybe not," says Roman. He means the traffic.

In the rear view mirror I can see a triad of eyes, nose and mouth, separate objects in constant animation. His mouth forms a kind of question mark when he is not speaking. His dark eyes scan me and the road, back and forth. In conversation, his nose twitches as if to manage opposite impulses of certainty and reflection like an emotional traffic light.

Roman is part Armenian, part Russian. He tells me he's American now. He's attached to Arrivals & Departures the way other immigrants live in their social clubs. He survived a brush with bankruptcy at the hands of a crooked gem importer, a fellow Russian ("Always the worst scammers.") and four years of college tuitions. Two kids: a son in software, and a daughter who wants to be an actress. He lives in Glendale but everyone in Los Angeles County remembers the accident.

Roman asks, "You know about tragedy last summer?"

He means the Accident, of course, not the death of my wife. Everyone's got something. Roman's no exception. He's going to tell me the story, but first he explains how he got to LA.

In 1990, not long before everything fell apart, Roman tried to leave the Soviet Union legally. His timing wasn't good. As an aspiring ex-citizen, he surrendered his passport. The loss of a passport prompted the termination of his job as a chemist and his wife's, who was a teacher. The family became a non-entity. But for a bureaucratic fumble, his army pension would have been cancelled, too. Once he pursued an exit visa, the state left him, not the other way around. Nationality–wise, he became the undead, on the border between the life he'd always known and the one he imagined in California. The better part of each day was spent in a line-up for yet another document. Roman was down to the rubles in his wallet when the August coup d'état took place. The day after Yeltsin hoisted himself atop a tank, Roman entered the American embassy with no domestic KGB agent in sight.

"Is not bad driving, but not for my kids."

Whenever the subject of their future comes up, he swats his bald pate as if they were right there in the front seat attempting to pluck the last of the grey hairs from between his ears. Road rage and chronically jammed freeways, the stuff of daily exasperation and accumulated stress, seem not to affect Roman. After all, he learned to drive in Afghanistan. One day soldiers, supplies the next. The kidnappings and ambushes by Pashtun warriors were stories told to Roman by soldiers passing through Kabul on their way home. Roman's battle was to arrive with full loads. Sometimes there was a convoy to protect him.

"Sometimes things fell off the truck." Little wink.

I like Roman. He's okay with the in-between stuff; he's learned the thing to dodge in life is the all-or-nothing approach, not the troubles. Tomorrow, Roman promises to get me back to LAX and after two months around the world, I'll soon be home.

The traffic is moving well along Lincoln Boulevard, past gun stores and gas stations, liquor stores and loan sharks. And rattan furniture retailers. I am beginning to wonder if while I was away bamboo hasn't made a massive comeback in America's rec rooms. In LA, it takes practice to discern nascent from dearly departed lifestyle trends. When I worked on beer accounts I used to study the boardwalks of Venice Beach and Santa Monica to "stay ahead of the curve." That was a lifetime ago.

We arrive at the Four Points. It is being renovated; they never tell you about that.

Between the revolving door and the cab are two heavyset Latinos, with smooth black hair and paint-spattered white shirts and trousers. They pull slowly on cigarettes. Their fingers are cupped like seashells, arranged for maximum surreptitious inhalation. They turn their heads away from the smoke plumes as if they had nothing to do with it. By the time Roman extracts my bag, the painters are gone, smoke and all, as if they'd never existed.

Inside, the desk clerk tells me that the noise and construction is evidence of the new owners' commitment to upgrade from Four Points to full Sheraton and not, as it feels to me and the Mexicana Airlines flight crew ahead, an unexpected annoyance.

My room is full of rattan furniture. At least the message light on the phone is not blinking. It's like the itch of a phantom limb, this feeling I should be meeting someone to review a casting tape or re-convince a client about a contentious TV script. The fiercest discussion I ever had was with a client from Switzerland who made chocolate bars and dog food. The shoot had gone well, including a tricky shot to make the dog food look good while sliding out of the can. We used a fork to get it into Fido's bowl. The client had a strong objection to the rough edit, my producer had called to say, but she didn't know why. We had to meet immediately or risk a costly re-shoot. For a moment I hoped the issue was the truly repulsive pack shot. He was ticked off about something.

"Where is the doggie spoon?" he demanded as if we had pulled a fast one.

Furtive glances around the boardroom. Doggie spoon? What's that? In Europe, there is no interspecies mixing of cutlery. You would never use the same fork as your dog. A doggie spoon maybe *de rigueur* in Zurich, but I explained it is quite unknown in Mississauga. I fought long and hard for the fork and in the end there was no re-shoot. Thomas Von Something-or-

Other went home unbowed. He had made his point and advertising's high standards for integrity and cultural meaning survived.

The last hotel of my world trip won't be remembered for its architecture. Like a lot of buildings in LA, it needs a coat of paint or maybe something more. Nevertheless, the Four Points robustly proclaims its economic advantages on a vibrantly coloured sign only a driver at fifty miles per hour could appreciate. Pedestrians do not stay in hotels.

LA is set up for trips between Points A and B. In between is immaterial. Roman's cab ride inured me to the city's decay but it's hard not to notice signs and billboards. Admonishments include cheap food, cheap cable and newer, cheaper cars. If all else fails, advertising advises, the indolent life you really deserve is a cheap flight away.

The sign outside the high school refers to upcoming graduation ceremonies as if it were a product launch. I wonder if the valedictorian will encourage the graduating class to live up to the school's "brand values."

I am on the sidewalk, walking east on Arizona Avenue and falling in step with teenagers who've drifted away from the school. I'm no longer in search of cultural cues for next summer's beer campaign but I do want to see what Roman was talking about. It's conspicuous to be a pedestrian in LA; only teenagers and the homeless resort to walking. Very occasionally it is fatal.

The retro style of Santa Monica High feels like the set of a movie, which in fact it has been in *Rebel Without a Cause* and *Fast Times at Ridgemount High*. Residents call it SAMOHI. It has 3,500 students tucked in behind their desks, some of whom will become celebrities. Presumably the glass cabinets outside the principal's office display photos of famous alumni like Robert Downey, Jr., Rob Lowe, and, the present-day James Dean, Sean Penn.

Likely Penn ducked class and hung out on Arizona just like these students. It's also possible that thirty years ago, Russell Weller, a reserved, church-going, fifty-seven-year-old literacy advocate, tutored Penn who attended SAMOHI between 1973 and 1978. On Arizona, where the Santa Monica Farmer's Market is held twice a week, it is striking to see homeless people pushing shopping carts in a shopping area and realize they're not shopping.

While Penn pursued marriage to and divorce from Madonna the Material Girl, lived in an Airstream trailer while estranged from his second wife, received better and better movie roles, notoriety for political activism, and finally an Oscar, Weller spent three decades uneventfully improving the reading skills of English students. In the panorama of his life, Weller's landmark was his appointment to the Santa Monica Library Board. Until the day of the Accident.

A breeze kicks litter on Arizona and cools my head. This is the exact spot where the unthinkable happened. On Wednesday, July 16, 2003, at 1:30 PM, vendors at the farmers' market were preparing to close for the day because it was raining. No one could remember that happening in July in a quarter century. Weller, eighty-six, was coming home from an errand at the post office in his burgundy Buick LeSabre and drove west on Arizona Avenue. He plowed through the temporary wooden bollards above the Third Street Promenade and drove the length of two city blocks through the middle of the market, killing two children, ten adults, and seriously injuring sixty others.

The tragedy started when Weller rear-ended another car, which had stopped for a pedestrian. The farmers' market has been a Santa Monica fixture for two decades but he told investigators he'd been surprised to see the road blocked. Mistaking the gas pedal for the brake, he accelerated toward the busy open-air market, covering a distance of 245 feet, hitting a pedestrian on crutches. Police said Weller had his "eyes open, hands on the steering wheel at the ten o'clock and two o'clock positions," and avoided parked cars on both sides as the car leveled stands and hurled pedestrians into the air. On impact the thuds were loud enough that bystanders thought they heard gunshots. Inexplicably, Weller accelerated to sixty miles per hour. Police reported that it "only slowed as a result of objects trapped beneath it, including a body." The car came to rest near Ocean Avenue and the air bag deployed, leaving Weller unharmed. The windshield crumpled like a wet shopping bag. One victim remained on the hood and a woman was found crushed underneath. It took less than a minute from normal to horrific.

Braham Manahedgi, fifty, exited a cheese shop just as Weller's car stopped right in front of him. Manahedgi had hiked for many years in the rough terrain of Southern California's wilderness areas. On weekends he volunteered in a 911-rescue unit at China Lake. On this day, there was no one to rescue. He was the first to speak to Weller opening the car door, cane in hand.

"His eyes were open and he was alive. I said, 'Do you know what the hell you did?' He said, 'No.'"

Police searching Weller's home for medication and evidence of his fitness to drive discovered Weller had recently "struck the back of his garage at least twice." Mary Roney, who lived two doors down from Weller and his wife for thirty years, said she knew of no health problems.

"A more careful, gentle, loving person you'll never find." She described her neighbour as being active in the community, including serving on a library board and tutoring students at

Santa Monica High School. Her husband Herb, chair of the Santa Monica College Board of Trustees, told the press, "He's just a person that you would want as a father, as a grandfather, and as a neighbour. He's a very, very nice person."

What are the odds?

By late afternoon, I snake and ladder back to the hotel. A Looney Bins garbage truck blows past me on an orange light at Wilshire. On Montana, I notice a poster in the window of an antique store, apparently re-opened after a long absence: "The tradition is back." Does tradition go away? A sign on a bus bench nearby reads: "Cremations with Dignity." Is there some other kind? I eat a bowl of *penne arrabiata* at Wolfgang Puck's. Not *the* Wolfgang Puck's, but a "value" version of his chain restaurant. This distinction would be lost on the contingent of homeless people socializing in the park beside the Catholic church, one block away.

Back at the rattan palace, everything's packed by the time NBC's *Nightly News* comes on. I graze the mini-bar. Clothes, sketchbooks, souvenirs are either check-in or carry-on depending on whether I'm prepared to lose a thing or not.

It's probably time to check into the status of my suspended self-employment. I call Frank, my production manager, at home. He tells me that a few weeks ago a competitor bought out one of my clients. My advertising assignment will be put out for tender, which is standard. Following a perfunctory review, we agree I will lose the account to another agency, which is also standard. All things considered, I'll be okay. I fall asleep thinking about going on to Japan to defer the end but I know it's time to close the circle.

To see myself as I really am and live in the world the way it really is, including the suicide and all the pain and questions it raised, I have followed a riddle back to the beginning.

Wherever you go, there you are.

In the morning, I head back to LAX. One last flight. I thank Roman for the story.

"Take care of yourself."

"Take care of yourself."

What else can we say?

" LIFE IS THE
DESTINATION. "
— Me.

TORONTO
CANADA
43

So Long

The terrible thing about the quest for truth is that you find it.
                                           —Remy de Gourmont

The one thing to do is quit before you die. That's always the smart move.
          —Gordon Hardman, competitor, Hardrock Hundred Race,
                  Silverton, CO. Finished seven times, quit six times.

IT'S A LONG WAY TO uncertainty, there and back.
     So long.
     The trip is over. I have said thanks and goodbye to my travel companions, the pen and the Voice. Trusting their intuition, I've given up daydreams. I will not become a wine label designer in New Zealand, a postage stamp merchant in Saint Lucia, a Hindu, a Buddhist, or an agnostic. To be myself after stalking myself has had all the relief of peace after war.
     So long.

To the secret that wasn't. It turns out the trip to find Erin's dark motives or life's hidden explanation for her death or to find some remote place to jettison grief never existed. It was a reconnaissance mission looking for me.

There will be things beyond my comprehension but now I see these future events and my self as elements, not flaws, in every picture.

Life is not fragile. It is unimaginably potent. I couldn't keep it bottled up, preserving it for another time. The pen saw to that, drawing on grief, letting everything in. I've stopped thrashing against time and that's as much grace as I could ever hope for.

What is astonishing about grief is that it can be an uplifting experience. It is intended, I have learned, to restore self. That it comes after a great loss disguises grief's meaning but not its power to make us attentive to our own depth and the profound connectedness of being human and here. It's not about atonement, but gratitude.

I'm home but in a sense I am still coming home. It was a powerful temptation to stay thirty thousand feet above life, safe in the bubble that carried me through three continents. But as soon as I decided it was time to come home, a second, significant event took place the night before I left Los Angeles for Toronto. I called my mother, the clearing house for all worthwhile news and the command central of my family. Instead, my sister picked up the phone and announced our mother hadn't passed her latest test, that her six-month chest scan was positive. Sylvia Mary Clewes died four months later.

So long.

I hold on to my pen. It has made some things visible and others sensible. If faith is a glimpse, rather than a complete vision, the increments of ink that come as written words or drawn shapes are tiny proofs that I'm on the right track. It seems so obvious now: life is the destination.

How we become ourselves appears to have something to do with consciously filling in the outlines imposed by life and death—and to approach each new circumstance with good intentions. Given a mundane need to earn a living, I went back to advertising. But I've had to rebalance my life, lose the old uses for it, recalibrate for the Voice as well as voice-overs. I've learned we're supposed to encounter light and dark and treat them with equanimity. This may be the start of an encounter with the divine or just a good drawing strategy.

In my car driving to see Sylvia on her last morning, I listened to the Great Western Orchestra playing Tchaikovsky's "Waltz of the Flowers" from *The Nutcracker Suite*. In defiance of fortified memories from childhood Christmases, harps, violins, and French horns suddenly slipped their moorings and in their places banjos, ukuleles, and harmonicas—instruments I never imagined could play classical music—were dealing elegantly with the lush theme, the lovely uplift of a three-quarter meter and the famous cadenza. It was an unthinkable rendition of my mother's favourite music.

So long.

I am hearing life for the first time all over again.

Acknowledgements

WITHOUT THE ENCOURAGEMENT from friends and family, this book would have been postcards read by mail sorting machines. I owe debts of gratitude to Ben McNally who believed in Lily before I did; Meg Taylor for finding a home for the story and especially Jonathan Schmidt, my editor, who asked only that I tell the truth. To Sherry and her family for their generosity. To my own family—Peter, Mary, Brian, Janet, Karyn, Meghan, Kyle and Sally— thank you for your constant encouragement.

Several people read the book along the way. I am grateful to everyone at Key Porter particularly Jordan Fenn and Anna Porter, Ingrid Paulson for her exquisite design, Marijke Friesen for polishing it so beautifully, and Carol Harrison for her painstaking copy edit. Enormous thanks are also due to Frank & Linda Clarke ("pleasure old boy"); Peter & Heather Kendall; Dave & Eddie Corner; Kara McIntosh; Jeff & Cherryl Collins; Andrew Freedman & Julie Martin; Doug Panton & Sylvie Daigneault; Sally and Jefferson Mappin; David Fleury; Archie Van Dyke; John Burghardt; Adrian DiCastri; Paul Hodgson; Greg Gatenby; Valerie Jacobs; Norman Simon; Brian and Barbara Chadbourne; Terry Iwaskiw & Sheila Cameron; David Logan; Delmarie Scherloski; Ann Bowman and, Eustace & Maria and Rosemary at Ladera. Finally, to Christine for understanding.

Permissions